D1092169

Date Due

Riverside City College Library
Riverside, California

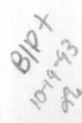

BIP+
10-19-73
972

HOBBES'S
SYSTEM OF IDEAS

Philosophy

Editor
PROFESSOR H. J. PATON
MA, FBA, D.Litt, LL.d.
*Emeritus Professor of Moral Philosophy
in the University of Oxford*

Hobbes's
System of Ideas

A STUDY IN
THE POLITICAL SIGNIFICANCE
OF PHILOSOPHICAL THEORIES

J. W. N. WATKINS

*Reader in the History of Philosophy
in the University of London*

HUTCHINSON UNIVERSITY LIBRARY

LONDON

LTD

, *W.1*

★

First published 1965

*This book has been set in Times New Roman,
printed in Great Britain on Smooth Wove paper
by The Anchor Press, Ltd., and bound by Wm.
Brendon & Son Ltd., both of Tiptree, Essex.*

Contents

References

The following abbreviations are used:

HOBBES:

EW   *The English Works of Thomas Hobbes*, edited by Sir William Molesworth, 11 vols., 1839–45.

De Cive   *Philosophical Rudiments concerning Government and Society*, 1651 (Hobbes's translation, with additions, of his *Elementa Philosophica De Cive*, 1647). References are to chapter and section.

De Corp *Elements of Philosophy: the first section, concerning Body* (a translation, approved by Hobbes, of *Elementorum Philosophiae Sectio Prima De Corpore*, 1655). References are to part, chapter and section.

El of L   *The Elements of Law*, edited by F. Tönnies, Cambridge University Press, 1928. (Contains *Human Nature* and *De Corpore Politico*, 1650. Appendix I consists of a previously unpublished 'Short Tract on First Principles'.) References are to part, chapter and section.

Lev   *Leviathan*, 1651. References are to the pages of the first edition (also given in the Oxford edition).

BACON:

Works   *The Works of Francis Bacon*, edited by J. Spedding, R. L. Ellis and D. D. Heath, 7 vols., 1857–9.

CUDWORTH:

TIS   *The True Intellectual System of the Universe*, edited by Thomas Birch, 4 vols., 1820.

DESCARTES:

PW   *Philosophical Works of Descartes*, translated by E. S. Haldane and G. R. T. Ross, 2 vols., 1931.

GALILEO:

DO   *Discoveries and Opinions of Galileo*, translated and introduced by Stillman Drake, 1957.

TCWS   *Dialogue Concerning the Two Chief World Systems —Ptolemaic and Copernican*, translated by Stillman Drake, foreword by Albert Einstein, California, 1953.

TNS   *Dialogues Concerning Two New Sciences*, translated by H. Crew and A. de Salvio, introduction by A. Favaro, 1914.

HARVEY:

Works   *The Works of William Harvey, M.D.*, translated by Robert Willis, M.D., 1847.

HUME:

Enquiries   *Enquiries Concerning The Human Understanding and Concerning The Principles of Morals*, edited by L. A. Selby-Bigge, 2nd edition, 1902.

Treatise   *A Treatise of Human Nature*, edited by L. A. Selby-Bigge, 1888.

LEIBNIZ:

G   C. I. Gerhardt, *Die philosophischen Schriften von Gottfried Wilhelm Leibniz*, 7 vols., 1875–90.

PPL   *Philosophical Papers and Letters*, translated and edited by L. E. Loemker, 2 vols., 1956. (I have sometimes preferred my own translation.)

In a run of references to the same work, the work's title is dropped after the first reference. References to Hobbes's writings are, where convenient, twofold: first to the individual book and second to the *English Works*. Thus '*De Corp* I, i, 1 & *EW* i, p. 1' means that the passage is in *De Corpore*, Part I, chapter i, section 1, and in *English Works*, volume i, page 1. Where practicable, references to other major philosophers follow a similar pattern.

Preface

This book is about Hobbes's ideas and certain logical connections between them. It is not biographical. The question it answers is, How much of Hobbes's *political* theory is implied by his *philosophical* ideas? The conclusion it reaches is that the essentials of his political theory are so implied. (In view of the widespread belief that all philosophical statements are morally and politically neutral, this conclusion is perhaps of some philosophical interest.) My accounts of the individual pieces of the Hobbesian jigsaw are fairly orthodox. There are a few problems of interpretation, mostly connected with Hobbes's theory of mind, which I think I have solved in a fresh way; and I think I have found out something about the historical relation between Leibniz's theory of matter and Hobbes's theory of mind. But if this book makes a contribution it is with respect to the fitting together of the pieces, rather than the pieces themselves.

With the notable exception of Michael Oakeshott's Introduction to *Leviathan*, most modern studies of Hobbes may be divided into two classes: those which do not assert that the pieces fit together, and those which assert that the pieces do not fit together. But Hobbes's contemporaries tended to regard his moral and political doctrines as part and parcel of his world-view.[1] What aroused their hostility was their realization that he was attempting to transform their God-supervised, man-oriented, law-bound and comfortably articulated cosmos into something quite alien: into a material expanse within which lonely individuals are driven by terror to manufacture a

[1] See S. I. Mintz, *The Hunting of Leviathan*, 1962, p. vii and *passim*.

Leviathan whose definitions will create an artificial morality for them, and whose sword will impose an artificial unity on them. I have tried to work out in some detail, and with a certain rigour, this older view of the connectedness of Hobbes's theories about nature, man and civil society.

One cannot arrive at a coherent view of an author's system merely by reading carefully everything he wrote. One has to try out provisional interpretations, modifying and developing them by repeatedly testing them against his writings, hoping to arrive eventually at a unified interpretation which seems to do justice to the main tendencies in his thinking. It is easier to test one's interpretation if rival interpretations have been published. These sharpen the issues and oblige one to attend to awkward passages. In this respect I have been fortunate: forceful interpretations, backed by genuine scholarship, and clashing with my own, have been advanced by Leo Strauss and Howard Warrender. It is from the two Hobbes scholars with whom I disagree most that I have learnt most, though what I learnt was not always what they taught. Since it is easier for a reader to appraise an interpretation when it is confronted with rival interpretations, I have brought our larger disagreements into the open.

I have attempted to assess the validity of only a few of the many controversial ideas of Hobbes considered here. To have attempted to assess them all would have made the book impossibly long. Systematic criticism is reserved till the concluding sections, and is mainly confined to Hobbes's political ideas.

The book was written during 1963, but I had been working on the ideas in it for a good many years. I published an article, 'Philosophy and Politics in Hobbes', in the *Philosophical Quarterly*, April 1955.[1] (This article contained at least one blunder: see below, pp. 140 f.) In 1960 I wrote what was intended as a chapter on Hobbes for a projected book on political philosophy. The chapter was to serve as a case-study to illustrate a general conception of political philosophy. However,

[1] To be re-published with minor alterations in *Hobbes Studies*, ed. K. C. Brown, 1965.

my friend Imre Lakatos became keen that I should turn it into a book; and his propagandist activities to this end led, indirectly, to my entirely re-writing it for Professor Paton's series. My hope is that in its latest form it will serve as a helpful introduction to Hobbes. Admittedly, it is an argumentative book organized around a controversial thesis; but the nature of the thesis ensures that most of Hobbes's main ideas should be considered; its controversial character will warn the reader unversed in Hobbes's writings that this book is no substitute for them, to which it gives ample references; and I have tried to write plainly and without presupposing any knowledge of Hobbes on the reader's part.

Over the 1960 version I had most valuable help from Joseph Agassi, and also from William Bartley who gave me many pages of closely typed and reasoned criticisms; I should also like to thank the members of his seminar at the Warburg Institute for their patient and helpfully critical reception of it during the Michaelmas term, 1962. Keith Brown made a number of beneficial criticisms.

The present version has benefited considerably from the criticisms of Kenneth Minogue and of H. J. Paton, the editor of this series. My largest debt is to Karl Popper. His has been the main influence on the viewpoint from which the book is written (as will be particularly apparent in §§ 3, 24, 28 and 32). He has also made a large number of criticisms, some small, some big, and all leading to improvements.

March 1964
London School of Economics and Political Science

I

Introduction

Hobbes's ideas on nature, man and civil society hang together, form a system. Within this system, controlling positions are occupied by a number of purely *philosophical* ideas. Moreover —and this is my main thesis—these philosophical ideas collectively imply enough of his *political* theory to provide a drastic solution for the political problems posed for him by the Puritan Rebellion.

We must begin, then, by considering Hobbes's reading of the Puritan Rebellion, to understand the desiderata which he wanted his political theory (or 'civil philosophy' as he called it) to meet. Then we must decide which of Hobbes's ideas should be counted as philosophical, and in what sense a philosophical idea can have political implications.

These preliminaries will occupy this chapter. In subsequent chapters various philosophical ideas of his will be examined and some of his more striking political ideas will be shown to be implications of them. These political implications will eventually be assembled, and will then be found to constitute a solution for his original political problems.

§ 1 *The Puritan Rebellion*

In 1639 the King's 'three kingdoms [were] flourishing in entire peace and universal plenty', according to the Earl of Clarendon[1] (at one time a friend, but afterwards a stern critic of Hobbes).

[1] *Life*, Oxford, 1857, i, p. 66.

Yet in 1642 civil war broke out, and in 1649 the King was beheaded. What caused an established political system to crack up? Clarendon himself hardly knew. He indicates the sort of factors which inclined men to side with King or Parliament once hostilities had broken out; but their outbreak itself 'appears to him', as a nineteenth-century critic put it, 'an impious, wicked, unnatural rebellion. . . . He views it with as much astonishment as horror.'[1] The only explanation he offers is a conspiracy-theory: he blames the rebellion on the treacherous schemings of 'ill men'.[2]

James Harrington, a contemporary of Clarendon and Hobbes, put forward a sociological explanation (in his *Oceana*, 1656). Its major premiss was that political power depends on military power which depends on economic power which depends on land-ownership, and its minor premiss was that, since the time of Henry VII, the ownership of land in England had become increasingly dispersed, a diminishing proportion being owned by the King and his natural allies, so that by 1640 the superstructure of royal political power had become topheavy and ready to collapse.

Hobbes's explanation was neither so impersonal as Harrington's nor so personal as Clarendon's. He attributed the deterioration to *ideas*—to wrong ideas, and especially to bad theology and bad philosophy. (Few men have been more impressed by the practical importance of ideas.)[3] For him the main cause of the Puritan Rebellion was Puritan ideology.

Hobbes's *Leviathan* (1651) was, in his own words, 'occasioned by the disorders of the present time'.[4] But it prescribes a cure, not just for these English disorders (or for contemporary political upheavals in other parts of Europe: as Christopher Hill has said, '1648, like 1848, was a year of revolutions').[5] It prescribes a universal cure for all revolution and civil war.

[1] J. F. Stephen, *Horae Sabbaticae*, 1892, i, p. 310.
[2] See his *Brief View and Survey of . . . Leviathan*, 1676, p. 54.
[3] See *De Cive*, Pref. & *EW* ii, pp. xi–xiii.
[4] *Lev*. p. 395 & *EW* iii, p. 713.
[5] Christopher Hill, *Puritanism and Revolution*, 1962, p. 133.

Hobbes's *Behemoth* was also concerned with these disorders; but whereas *Leviathan* is prescriptive, *Behemoth* is descriptive. It traces the changing location of political power in England between 1640 and 1660, and investigates the causes of the King's loss of sovereignty. Its sub-title is: 'The History of the Causes of the Civil Wars of England . . .' 'Behemoth' stands for the Long Parliament which sat from 1640 until Cromwell dissolved the surviving Rump of it in 1653, and which was restored in 1660. 'Leviathan' stands for a sovereign power of the kind which is necessary to prevent rebellion and civil war. In the Old Testament Behemoth is a powerful sea-monster: 'his bones are as strong pieces of brass; his bones are like bars of iron';[1] but he is less formidable than Leviathan: *he* 'esteemeth iron as straw, and brass as rotten wood'.[2] Moreover, as Hobbes himself pointed out, Leviathan is there said by God to be 'King of all the children of pride'.[3]

In *Behemoth* Hobbes gave both an immediate cause of the civil wars and a more underlying cause. The immediate cause was the King's assent, in 1641, to an Act whereby Parliament could not be dissolved without its own consent. Hobbes wrote as a staunch Royalist; but he does not hide his conviction that in doing this the King committed a grievous error: he allowed a rival power to become irremovable. Henceforth there 'was a divided power, in which there could be no peace'.[4]

But the King signed away his sovereignty only under heavy pressure; and this insurrectionary pressure was, according to Hobbes, ideologically generated. Among the subversive doctrines which he singled out as primarily responsible were these: that private men are judges of good and evil; that it is a sin to

---

[1] *Job* xl, 18.   [2] xli, 27.

[3] *Lev* pp. 166–7 & *EW* iii, p. 307. For the significance of the title, *Leviathan*, see Leo Strauss, *The Political Philosophy of Hobbes*, 1936, p. 13. For a modern account of Hebrew myths concerning Leviathan and Behemoth see Robert Graves and Raphael Patai, 'Some Hebrew Myths and Legends', *Encounter* 113, February 1963.

[4] *EW* vi, p. 319; and see pp. 257 and 310–11; see also *Lev* p. 93 & *EW* iii, p. 168. The Act is given in *Constitutional Documents of the Puritan Revolution*, ed. S. R. Gardiner, 1906, pp. 158–9.

do something against one's private conscience; that a man's private conscience may be supernaturally inspired;[1] and that the sovereign power may be limited or divided.[2] Such doctrines were the stock-in-trade of pulpit-preachers in the 1640's; but they had been brewed in the universities, which were therefore 'the core of the rebellion', a Trojan horse within the nation.[3]

Civil war due to divided authority, and divided authority due to ideological disputes—that, in brief, was Hobbes's reading of the Puritan Rebellion. This reading created the following desiderata for his civil philosophy:

(1) He must show the need for a political *sovereign*, undivided and unrestricted, obedience to whom is the citizen's overriding duty.

(2) To clinch this he should show that what *makes* anything a duty is its being commanded by a sovereign authority. To rebut the Puritan revolutionaries effectively, Hobbes wanted to show that any law is necessarily just and that it is impossible to have a duty to disobey one's sovereign.

(3) Moreover, Hobbes should, if possible, *demonstrate* all this. An argument which purported to show men that they must obey their sovereign, but which (like James VI's *True Law of Free Monarchies*) was itself one more inconclusive and controversial harangue, would merely add fuel to the flames it was intended to put out. Hobbes complained of his predecessors:

> those men who have written . . . of moral philosophy, or of policy, government, and laws, whereof there be infinite volumes, have been so far from removing doubt and controversy in the questions they have handled, that they have very much multiplied the same.[4]

---

[1] Thus the authors of *The Case of the Army* met the charge 'that we are transgressors of all order and form' with the claim that they acted from 'obligations upon our consciences (written naturally by the finger of God in our hearts)' (quoted in A. S. P. Woodhouse, *Puritanism and Liberty*, 1938, p. 436-7 n.).

[2] See *Lev* pp. 168–70 & *EW* iii, pp. 310–13.

[3] *EW* vi, pp. 213 and 233–6; and *Lev* pp. 179–80 & *EW* iii, pp. 330–2.

[4] *El of L* I, xiii, 3 & *EW* iv, p. 73.

A civil philosophy which satisfied these desiderata could be effectively taught at the universities,[1] from whence knowledge of it would spread, until all ranks of Englishmen understood their duty; then there would be peace, and security for 'commodious living'.

§ 2 *Philosophical ideas*

For Hobbes, as for most of his contemporaries, 'philosophy' was a compendious name for all kinds of rational or scientific enquiry.[2] He divided his own 'philosophical' writings into three main sections: natural philosophy, moral philosophy and civil philosophy; and he testified that in the event the last was published first, and is independent of the other two:

> I was studying philosophy for my mind sake, and I had gathered together its first elements in all kinds; and having digested them into three sections by degrees, I thought to have written them, so as in the first I would have treated of *body* and its general properties; in the second of *man* and his special faculties and affections; in the third, of *civil government* and the duties of subjects. . . . It so happened in the interim, that my country, some few years before the civil wars did rage, was boiling hot with questions concerning the rights of dominion and the obedience due from subjects . . .; and was the cause which, all those other matters deferred, ripened and plucked from me this third part. Therefore it happens, that *what was last in order, is yet come forth first in time. And the rather, because I saw that, grounded on its own principles sufficiently known by experience, it would not stand in need of the former sections.*[3]

This sounds inimical to the thesis of this book; but it is not really so. The premisses of his civil philosophy were psychological principles; and he was saying that these principles do

[1] *El of L* II, ix, 8 & *EW* iv, p. 219. Things turned out differently. Instead of being made a set book, *Leviathan* was burnt at Oxford. If it had been written today, it would probably have been refused a review in *Mind*.

[2] 'Now look, how many sorts of things there are, which properly fall within the cognizance of human reason; into so many branches does the tree of philosophy divide itself' (*De Cive* Ep. Ded. & *EW* ii, p. iii).

[3] Pref. & pp. xix–xx, my italics.

not need to be derived from physical principles. One might suppose that this hardly needed saying; but Hobbes needed to say it because he believed that it is possible, in principle at least, to derive psychological principles from physical principles. He was a materialist. He regarded so-called mental activities—thinking, wanting and so on—as a subtle kind of incipient movement within the person's body (see below, § 25). When he spoke of them as *motions* of the mind he was not speaking metaphorically. He held that, once natural philosophy has established the general principles of motion, moral philosophy should investigate the causes and principles of these special motions:

> After *physics* [or natural philosophy] we must come to *moral philosophy*; in which we are to consider the motions of the mind, namely, *appetite, aversion,* . . . &c; what causes they have, and of what they be causes.[1]

Civil philosophy, however, need not be held up until moral philosophy has completed its task. To arrive at an understanding of the motions of the mind by a long and complicated process of 'ratiocination' from more fundamental physical principles is a needlessly roundabout procedure; for there is another, and much easier, method, namely introspection:

> *Civil* and *moral philosophy* do not so adhere to one another, but that they may be severed. For the causes of the motions of the mind are known, not only by ratiocination, but also by the experience of every man that takes the pains to observe those motions within himself.[2]

It is no part of the thesis of this book that Hobbes deduced his psychological principles from physical principles (though in Chapter VI it will be maintained that Hobbes's materialism gave a distinctive twist to psychological commonplaces). Hobbes himself said that 'the principles of natural science . . . cannot teach us our own nature'.[3]

Conceptions of philosophy have altered significantly since

[1] *De Corp* I, vi, 6 & *EW* i, p. 72.   [2] I, vi, 7 & p. 73.
[3] *Lev* p. 191 & *EW* iii, p. 354.

the seventeenth century. Hobbes's definition makes it well-nigh indistinguishable from what we would now call science:

> *Philosophy* is such knowledge of effects or appearances, as we acquire by true ratiocination from the knowledge we have first of their causes or generation: and again, of such causes or generations as may be from knowing first their effects.[1]

Elsewhere, Hobbes defines 'philosophy' as *the knowledge of natural causes*.[2] But this definition hardly accommodates what are regarded today as Hobbes's most characteristic philosophical ideas. These are mostly interpretative principles rather than scientific theories. Thus his *materialism* interprets thinking and feeling, like blinking and kneeling, as bodily activities; but it does not attempt to explain, in terms of people's bodily constitutions, why they mostly think that $2+2=4$ or that London is the capital of England. His *determinism* interprets every change as causally determined; but it does not offer a causal explanation for particular kinds of change, nor does it enable us to predict any new effects. His nominalism interprets words like 'man' and 'mortal' on the analogy of proper names, but it hardly provides a causal explanation for the existence of either common or proper names. Nor does his definition cover an enquiry into the *methods of* 'philosophy' (in his sense) itself. Yet a considerable part of *De Corpore*, Hobbes's major philosophical work, is concerned with method. Indeed, it is doubtful whether this work contains *any* 'philosophy' on this definition (though his rather desultory discussions in Part IV of the causes of ice, lightning and thunder, etc., might just qualify).

In Hobbes's day two distinctions which are now fairly commonplace were not drawn sharply: that between *cosmology* and *epistemology*, and that between a *scientific* and a *metaphysical* cosmological theory. By a cosmological theory I mean a theory about the external world, or some aspect or part of it. Gilbert's magnetic theory, the astronomical theories of Copernicus and Kepler, and Galileo's theory of motion were all, in this sense, cosmological theories. By an epistemological

---

[1] *De Corp* I, i, 2 & *EW* i, p. 3.   [2] *EW* vii, p. 71.

theory I mean a theory about our knowledge (or opinions) about the external world. (Cosmology, one might say, has an extraverted and epistemology a more introverted orientation.) An epistemological theory will, typically, be a theory about how knowledge begins, the methods by which these beginnings are (or should be) cultivated, the certain or probable or conjectural status of the conclusions thereby arrived at, and so on. Since human knowledge and human language involve each other, an epistemological theory is almost bound to comprise some theory of the language in which we describe the world. And an epistemological theory may be extended to comprehend moral ideas and the language in which they are expressed.

Near the end of the seventeenth century the separation of cosmology and epistemology was effected by Locke. He disclaimed any intention of adding to the cosmological knowledge which the great scientific master-builders (Boyle, Huygens, Newton) have given us. He thought that it was in vain for us to 'let loose our thoughts into the vast ocean of being' unless we first 'take a survey of our own understandings, examine our own powers, and see to what things they were adapted'.[1]

Hobbes's position was closer to that of his near-contemporaries, Bacon and Descartes. Both these men were deeply concerned with epistemological (or methodological) questions, but this was because their aim was the construction of a new, and true, *cosmology*, and they considered it hopeless to attempt this without first mastering the methods by which alone (or so they believed) it could be done. They wanted to travel—indeed, to arrive. They agreed that travel-preparations were necessary, but they regarded these as the essential first stage of the journey (though Bacon got permanently delayed at this stage). For them, epistemology was *part and parcel* of cosmology.

Hobbes's position was similar, except that he wanted to construct not only a theory of the physical world but a theory of society too; and he did not delay too long over his travel-preparations. Both in *De Corpore*, his main work in natural philosophy, and in *Leviathan*, his main work in civil philo-

[1] *Essay Concerning Human Understanding*, 1690, I, i, 7.

sophy, epistemological ideas are presented in the opening chapters as part and parcel of the whole theory.

This gives us one uncontroversial terminological convention. Although he did not draw the distinction, or even use the word 'epistemology', we shall count as 'philosophical' those of his ideas which are, from a modern standpoint, epistemological. Unfortunately, it is not possible to lay down a completely uncontroversial convention as to which of his cosmological ideas should be regarded as metaphysical and therefore as philosophical. There is much disagreement among non-positivists about what metaphysical ideas are, and positivists deny their existence. Let us say that a cosmological theory is metaphysical if it makes a factual assertion about the world which, however, is not open to empirical test.[1] Positivists will say that if it is not open to empirical test, it is not a factual assertion. But this is incorrect if there are cosmological theories which, though not empirically testable, *conflict* with hypotheses which *are* empirically testable. (No conflict without content.) Now Hobbes advanced several cosmological theories of just this nature. A conspicuous example is his proposition that all changes are caused by *push*, by one body touching or pressing against another (see below, pp. 43 f.). This conflicts with the theory that every body exerts an *attractive* force (varying with the masses of the bodies and inversely with the square of the distance) on bodies *at a distance* from it. This latter theory (in conjunction with certain subsidiary assumptions) is empirically testable; hence Hobbes's conflicting theory is factual. But as he stated it, it is untestable. It tells us that a falling stone falls because *something* is pushing it downwards, but it does not tell us what this something is, nor does it say that we should detect it if only we would examine the stone and its immediate environment carefully.

Another example from Hobbes's cosmology is his proposition

[1] I am drawing, in what follows, on a theory of metaphysical statements I have developed in: *Philosophy*, April 1957; *Mind*, July 1958; *Brit. Jour. Phil. of Science*, February 1960; and in a paper in *The Critical Approach to Science and Philosophy*, ed. M. Bunge, 1964.

that 'all motion has some effect upon all matter whatsoever'[1]—the skipping of a flea is propagated to the Indies,[2]
though it may pass undetected there. This proposition conflicts
with Max Planck's theory of the elementary quantum of action.
So Hobbes's proposition is factual. But it is also untestable;
observations, which are always a little rough and inexact,
could never establish that a certain movement had *absolutely* no
effect on a certain piece of matter.

In light-hearted moments I call those cosmological theories
which assert the existence of something which may elude our
attempts to detect it, *haunted-universe doctrines*. In the present
study, those of Hobbes's ideas which have this character will
be counted as metaphysical and philosophical.

§ 3   *The idea of a system of ideas*

We shall be primarily concerned with Hobbes's *ideas* and their
connections, rather than with the order in which he thought of
them (though this latter topic will be touched on in Chapter
II). There are important differences between ideas and the
thinking which produced them. If a minute-by-minute trans-
cript could somehow have been kept of all the thinking which
went into *Leviathan* it would no doubt have filled many hun-
dreds of volumes well-nigh impossible to read through.
Hobbes did much of that thinking in Paris; but the ideas in
Leviathan do not have a Parisian flavour. Hobbes stopped
thinking on 4 December 1679; but the ideas he gave us did not
go out of existence on that day. I shall argue that some of his
political ideas are implied by some of his philosophical ideas;
I shall not argue that his political *thinking* was governed by his
philosophical thinking.

An idea may be regarded as a sort of precipitate of the
thinking which went into it; but it also transcends that thinking.
It has infinitely many logical consequences, only a finite

---

[1] *De Corp* IV, xxvii, 8 & *EW* i, p. 455.
[2] This phrase was coined by Hobbes's opponent, Wallis; see *EW* vii,
p. 268.

number of which can have been consciously thought of by its author.[1] Some of its unconsidered consequences may be important. (A recipe for finding commonplace ideas with impressive implications is this. Take some powerful new scientific theory which has recently led to a striking new prediction. Formulate all the premisses used in the derivation of this prediction. Among these there will almost certainly be some commonplaces known long before the new theory was invented. Call one of these p, call the conjunction of all the other premisses q, and call the prediction r. Then an important and hitherto unconsidered implication of p is: if q, then r.)

Again, there may be logical relations between a man's ideas which do not correspond to any psychological relations between the bouts of thinking which led respectively to those ideas —logical relations of which, indeed, he may be unaware. An artificial example: Aubrey says that Hobbes

> walked much and contemplated, and he had in the head of his staffe a pen and inke-horne, carried alwayes a note-booke in his pocket, and as soon as a thought darted, he presently entred it into this booke, or otherwise he might perhaps have lost it.[2]

Imagine that one morning, reflecting on Charles I's execution, he entered the thought that all kings are mortal in his book; that afternoon, reflecting that men are but machines and that machines wear out, he entered the conclusion that all men are mortal; that evening, reflecting on Charles I's mistake in assenting to the Non-Dissolution Bill, he reflected that kings are but fallible humans, and entered this. (Desultory reflections; perhaps he was feeling off-colour today.)

From his notebook jottings we could now pick out a proposition with the logical structure of a syllogism: *All kings are men; all men are mortal/all kings are mortal.* But it would be wrong to say that we imagined Hobbes *thinking* syllogistically:

---

[1] A logical consequence of any given proposition p is: $[q \supset (p \supset r)] \supset (q \supset r)$; and there will be infinitely many propositions which could properly be substituted for q and r.

[2] John Aubrey, *Brief Lives*, ed. A. Clark, 1898, i, pp. 334–5.

what led him to reflect that all kings are mortal was the thought of Charles I's execution. And although it is improbable, he *might* not have noticed that these three ideas could be recast in a syllogistic pattern. An author of a system of ideas is a considerable authority on it, but he is bound to be unaware of, and may even be mistaken about, some of its ramifications and logical inter-connections.

The notion of a system of ideas which transcends the thinking behind it is illustrated rather strikingly by Euclid's *Elements* (a book which had a large influence on Hobbes). Euclid composed this work from various sources; yet it is a system of ideas *par excellence*, and many things can be said of it which cannot be said of the thinking either of those ancient geometers or even of Euclid himself. For instance, its relations to various non-Euclidean systems of geometry can be described; proofs of its consistency may be attempted;[1] and so on.

Since a system of ideas has indefinitely many ramifications, reconstructions of it will always be partial. Only *a* reconstruction of Hobbes's ideas will be attempted in this book. A word, now, about the sort of connections we shall consider.

A philosophical proposition cannot by itself entail a proposition having a political content which the former lacks. But the introduction of a philosophical theory p into an existing circle of statements q may make it possible to derive a new political conclusion r; in which case p implies that if q then r. Moreover, if r is controversial, whereas q consists of uncontroversial background assumptions (for instance, that men live in proximity to one another, that their resources are scarce, that it is physically possible for one man to kill another), then the philosophical idea bears the chief responsibility for the political conclusion, and the latter may be said, by a pardonable ellipsis, to be an *implication* of the philosophical idea. It is with this sort of objective connection that we shall mainly be concerned.

[1] Imre Lakatos points out that the problem of consistency did not arise while Euclid's system was regarded as a system of *truths*, between which there can be no inconsistencies (*Proc. Arist. Soc.* 1962, suppl. vol. xxxvi, pp. 158, 171).

One way in which such implications may occur deserves special mention. Many of Hobbes's philosophical ideas have what is sometimes called a 'second-order' status. A second-order statement says something general about a whole class of (first-order) statements. For example, the law of evidence has a second-order status *vis-à-vis* statements made by witnesses in law-courts. It does not *entail* any of them, but it has important implications for them. Again, a methodological theory may have important implications at the scientific level. If it says, for example, that a simpler scientific theory is preferable, other things being equal, to a less simple one, it may, in a particular scientific context, imply that theory A is preferable to theory B. We shall find that some of Hobbes's methodological ideas have implications in a rather similar way at the political level.

Although this book is an essay in logical reconstruction its approach will not be unhistorical. It is, after all, *Hobbes*'s ideas whose organization we shall investigate; and in trying to establish what a man's ideas are, one should use any available information about his problems and intentions and political and intellectual situation, about his contemporaries and their readings of him, and so on. As Hobbes himself remarked,

> it must be extreme hard to find out the opinions and meanings of those men that are gone from us long ago, and have left us no other signification thereof but their books; which cannot possibly be understood without history enough to discover those afore-mentioned circumstances.[1]

Many Hobbes scholars have concluded that his civil philosophy is not related in any interesting way to his philosophy.[2]

---

[1] *El of L* I, xiii, 8 & *EW* iv, p. 75.

[2] See, for example: G. C. Robertson, *Hobbes*, 1901, p. 57; A. E. Taylor, *Hobbes*, 1908, p. 44; John Laird, *Hobbes*, 1934, pp. 244–5; S. P. Lamprecht's Introduction to *De Cive*, N.Y., 1949, p. xvii; B. E. Jessup, 'Relation of Hobbes's Metaphysics to his Theory of Value', *Ethics*, April 1948, p. 216. Leo Strauss's *The Political Philosophy of Hobbes*, 1936, and Howard Warrender's *The Political Philosophy of Hobbes*, 1957, both of which uphold (though in very different ways) the autonomy of Hobbes's moral and political theory, will be discussed in § 5 and §§ 16–18 respectively.

I suspect that three main factors have encouraged this. First, they have tended to look for some simple linear connection between his philosophy and the premisses of his civil philosophy. Second, they have tended to identify Hobbes's 'philosophy' with his materialism, so that their question became: Does Hobbes's materialism entail the psychological premisses of his civil philosophy? And to this the answer is surely, No. Third, they have tended to suppose that the answer to the whole question was given by Hobbes himself when he said that the third section of his philosophy came first and does not need the other two.

We shall outflank the first two obstacles by using a wider net to catch Hobbes's philosophical ideas and by looking for more roundabout connections between these and his political ideas. As to the third: Hobbes said, not that he started philosophizing after he had completed his civil philosophy, but that he *deferred* his more philosophical work so that he could complete his civil philosophy first. We will now investigate what came first in his thinking.

II

Early Political and Scientific Thinking

It has sometimes been suggested that Hobbes took to philosophy after he had worked out his civil philosophy. The excellent Hobbes scholar, G. C. Robertson, wrote:

> In truth, however, the whole of his political doctrine . . . has little appearance of having been thought out from the fundamental principles of his philosophy. . . . It doubtless had its main lines fixed when he was still a mere observer of men and manners, and not yet a mechanical philosopher.[1]

This view, though strictly irrelevant, is likely to engender psychological resistance to the main thesis of this book, and it can now be refuted with the help of an important piece of evidence which came to light when the main text of Robertson's book was finished. A refutation of it will at the same time provide a preliminary survey of some of Hobbes's key philosophical ideas and an indication of some of their political implications.

§ 4   *History, geometry and motion*

Hobbes's earliest known political work—his *Thucydides* as I will call it—was his introduction to his translation of Thucydides' *History of the Peloponnesian War*. Hobbes published this in 1629. He completed the first version of his civil philosophy,

[1] George Croom Robertson, *Hobbes*, 1901, p. 57. (Robertson's book was first published in 1886.)

27

The Elements of Law, in 1640.[1] During 1629–31 he went on a continental tour which proved an intellectual turning-point. He discovered Euclid, and was bowled over:

> He was . . . 40 yeares old before he looked on geometry; which happened accidentally. Being in a gentleman's library. . . , Euclid's *Elements* lay open, and 'twas the 47 *El libri* I. He read the proposition. 'By G——,' sayd he, (He would now and then sweare, by way of emphasis), 'this is impossible!' So he reads the demonstration of it, which referred him back to such a proposition; which proposition he read. That referred him back to another, which he also read. *Et sic deinceps*, that at last he was demonstratively convinced of that trueth. This made him in love with geometry.[2]

Thus Hobbes learnt that a proposition whose truth by no means leaps to the eye, or which is even counter-intuitive, may nevertheless be found to follow, by a chain of deductions, from propositions which seem obviously true. In proving Pythagoras's startling theorem, Euclid only invites us to attend to logical consequences of propositions which we 'knew already' in the sense that, although we may have been unaware of them, we were bound to assent to them if they were presented to us. In the language of Plato's *Meno*,[3] Euclid only 'reminds' us of what we had 'forgotten'. To do this became (as we shall see in § 14) Hobbes's aim in his civil philosophy.

On this journey, also, Hobbes was seized by the idea that all the observable variety of nature is the result of *motion*, and that sense-experience itself is a kind of motion. This idea goes back

---

[1] First published in 1650 in two parts entitled *Human Nature* and *De Corpore Politico* respectively. The 'Epistle Dedicatory' is dated 9 May 1640. See the Preface by F. Tönnies, dated March 1889, to his edition of *The Elements of Law*.

[2] John Aubrey, *Brief Lives*, ed. A. Clark, i, p. 332.

[3] In this dialogue, 'Socrates' claims to get an unlettered slave-boy to replace his initial erroneous opinion about how to construct a square twice the area of a given square with a correct opinion, *merely by asking questions*—by eliciting what the slave-boy, without realizing it, already knows.

to the Greek atomists, but Hobbes seems to have arrived at it independently.

Thus around 1630 Hobbes fell in love with the Euclidean method of demonstration and with the idea of motion. The immediate outcome was a 'Short Tract on First Principles', which expounds a mechanistic metaphysics in Euclidean style. (This is the important piece of evidence I mentioned earlier.) It was discovered, and given this title, by F. Tönnies (who published it as Appendix I to his edition of *The Elements of Law*). He believed it to have been written around 1630 because Hobbes, in a letter dated 1646, dedicating to the Marquis of Newcastle a treatise on optics, said that what he had now written was derived from some ideas which he had put forward 'about 16 years since'.[1] Brandt, while allowing that the *Tract* (as I shall call it) *might* have been written as late as 1636, concludes 'that much speaks in favour of the date 1630 stated by Tönnies'.[2] All that matters here is that the *Tract* was written after *Thucydides* and before *The Elements of Law*, which no one disputes.

The thesis of this chapter (which is subsidiary to the main thesis of the book) is this. Of the two main political ideas of his *Thucydides*, one—the inductivist approach commended there— was soon repudiated by Hobbes, while the other—monarchism —came to occupy a subordinate position in his system; whereas all but one of the main ideas of the *Tract* came to occupy pretty central positions. Moreover, these philosophical ideas have some interesting political implications which became apparent in *The Elements of Law*. In other words, Hobbes was a mechanical philosopher before the main lines of his political doctrine were fixed, and his early philosophizing spilt over into his political theorizing. I will start by considering an opposed thesis.

---

[1] *EW* vii, p. 468.

[2] Frithiof Brandt, *Thomas Hobbes' Mechanical Conception of Nature*, 1928, p. 55. The first chapter of this excellent book is devoted to the *Tract*.

§ 5   *The Strauss thesis*

In *The Political Philosophy of Hobbes* (1936) Leo Strauss gave
Robertson's view an interesting twist and elaborated it into a
major reinterpretation of Hobbes. The twist was this: Hobbes's
political thinking came to be powerfully affected, but *adversely*,
by his subsequent philosophizing. More specifically: Hobbes
was originally, and always remained essentially, a humanist and
a moralist; but his middle-aged conversion to Euclideanism and
to the Galilean scientific tradition tempted him to try to under-
pin his original psychological and moral insights by 'basing'
them upon an alien, mechanistic theory of nature.

> The temptation to take this way could hardly be resisted. As
> traditional moral and political philosophy was, to some extent,
> based on traditional metaphysics, it seemed necessary, when
> traditional metaphysics were replaced by modern natural science,
> to base the new moral and political philosophy on the new
> science.[1]

The result (according to Strauss) was unfortunate. His civil
philosophy could not really be accommodated within the new
scientific tradition which had repudiated anthropomorphism
and teleology, and could therefore 'contribute nothing to the
understanding of things human, to the foundation of morals
and politics'.[2] The original moral and political insights were
compromised; but they were never abandoned:

> there was no change in the *essential* content of the argument and
> aim of Hobbes's political philosophy from the introduction to his
> translation of Thucydides up to the latest works.[3]

Forcing this essential content into an alien scientific context
bred 'numerous contradictions':

> There are but few of his most important and characteristic asser-
> tions which are not contradicted, either directly or by the denial
> of their obvious consequences, somewhere in his works.[4]

---

[1] p. xiii.   [2] *loc. cit.*   [3] p. 112, my italics.   [4] p. xiv.

This is a disheartening view. The political content of *Thucydides* is meagre. Who would care to read *Leviathan* if it consisted of this meagre core wrapped in a tissue of 'astonishing discrepancies', 'still more astonishing obscurities' and 'logical defects'?[1] But what, for Strauss, is this essential content? It is, he says, Hobbes's realization that *vanity* is 'the root of all evil',[2] whereas *fear* is the origin of justice, virtue and, ultimately, civilization.

> The moral and humanist antithesis of fundamentally unjust vanity and fundamentally just fear of violent death is the basis of Hobbes's political philosophy.[3]

For my part, I believe that the roles played by vanity and fear in Hobbes's scheme are indeed important (see p. 118 below). But the claim that this vanity/fear antithesis was *fundamental* can be criticized *via* Strauss's further claim that it led straight to another major antithesis, namely Hobbes's anti-democracy and pro-monarchy attitude. Call Hobbes's vanity/fear antithesis *A* and his democracy/monarchy antithesis *B*. If *A* were fundamental in Hobbes's political philosophy, and if *A* led to *B*, then if Hobbes regarded anything as proved or demonstrated within his political philosophy, he should surely have so regarded *B*. Indeed, Strauss claims that Hobbes proved *B* by *A* when he first stated the essence of his political philosophy in *Thucydides*.[4]

Yet nearly twenty years later, in the Preface to *De Cive*, Hobbes explicitly conceded that *B* alone was not demonstrated: 'though I have endeavoured, by arguments . . . , to gain a belief in men, that monarchy is the most commodious government', yet this 'one thing alone I confess in this whole book not to be demonstrated, but only probably stated';[5] and in *Thucydides* he had come nowhere near *proving* the superiority of monarchy, though he made his preference for monarchy plain.[6]

[1] p. 12.   [2] p. 111.   [3] pp. 27–8.
[4] p. 110.   [5] *EW* ii, p. xxii.
[6] *EW* viii, pp. xvi–xvii.

If we suspend judgement about what are the 'essentials' of Hobbes's civil philosophy and about whether any influence of his other ideas on his civil philosophy was adverse or not, Strauss's view provides encouraging support for our thesis. According to Strauss, Hobbes's philosophical, mathematical and scientific views had a large (if adverse) influence on large (if inessential) parts of his civil philosophy. For example, his Euclideanism and desire to emulate Galileo led him to replace the historical method of *Thucydides* by a new method which, Strauss allowed, had a considerable—if easily exaggerated—influence on his political philosophy:

> According to his [Hobbes's] own statements, his achievement in political philosophy was made possible by the application of a new method, the method by which Galileo raised physics to the rank of a science. In conformity with this method, which is called the 'resolutive-compositive', the given political facts . . . are analysed . . . and what was at first an 'irrational' whole is 'rationalised'. It would thus seem that the characteristic contents of Hobbes's political philosophy—the absolute priority of the individual to the State, the conceptions of the individual as asocial, of the relation between the state of nature and the State as an absolute antithesis, and finally of the State itself as Leviathan—[are] determined by and, as it were, implied in the method.[1]

(We shall take this matter up in Chapter IV.) Strauss further allowed that Hobbes's

> criticism of aristocratic virtue and his denial of any gradation in mankind gains certainty only through his conception of nature, according to which there is no order, that is, no gradation in nature.[2]

(We shall take this up in § 22.) And he agreed that Hobbes's denial that there are, by nature, any natural moral standards was underwritten by his materialist metaphysics.[3]

These may seem considerable concessions, in view of Strauss's main thesis; but they were more than counterbalanced, in his view, by a deeper consideration: whatever

[1] p. 2.   [2] p. 167.   [3] p. 165.

influence on his political philosophy it may have had, Hobbes's scientific metaphysics was itself, according to Strauss, the outcome of Hobbes's prior interest in things human and moral:

> Hobbes's turn to natural science is to be explained by his interest not so much in nature as in man, in self-knowledge of man. . . .

This may look like claiming that a botanist's turn to zoology is to be explained by his interest not so much in animals as in plants; but Strauss had an ingenious justification for his claim: Hobbes's

> scientific explanation of sense-perception is characterized by the fact that it interprets perception of the higher senses by the sense of touch; and the preference for the sense of touch which this presupposes is already implied in Hobbes's original view of the fundamental significance of the antithesis between vanity and fear.[1]

I take it that Strauss meant this: vanity typically involves visual imagery—we *picture* ourselves in flattering situations—whereas bodily fear is typically aroused by the prospect of being struck: vanity is primarily associated with sight, fear with touch; being anti-vanity and pro-fear, Hobbes preferred touch to sight; and this moral preference inspired him to work out a metaphysics which would make touch fundamental, and interpret seeing as a kind of touching.

Now it is quite true that Hobbes interpreted seeing as a kind of touching, in accordance with his push-theory of causation (see below, pp. 108–9). But this does not mean that he *preferred* touch to sight. (Also in accordance with this push-theory, he interpreted all pulling as a kind of pushing[2]—which does not imply that he preferred wheelbarrows to hand-carts.) And as a matter of fact, he did not prefer touch to sight. Optics was an abiding interest of his; and in the letter to the Marquis of

---

[1] p. 166.

[2] See *De Corp* III, xxii, 12 & *EW* i, pp. 343–4; the marginal summary is: 'All traction is pulsion.'

B

Newcastle mentioned above (p. 29), he commends optics on the ground that it is concerned with 'the noblest of the senses, *vision*'.[1] Hobbes preferred sight to touch.

§ 6   *Repudiation of inductivism*

While the preference for monarchy displayed in Hobbes's *Thucydides* did persist into his later political writings (though it came to occupy a subsidiary position), he soon discarded the other main idea of that work, namely that it is from a study of *history* that men should learn to conduct themselves rationally:

> The principal and proper work of history [is] to instruct and enable men, by the knowledge of actions past, to bear themselves prudently in the present and providently towards the future.[2]

Hobbes added:

> men profit more by looking on adverse events, than on prosperity; . . . men's miseries do better instruct, than their good success.[3]

At this early period Hobbes seems to have felt that the examination of particular past actions and their (happy or, more especially, unhappy) outcomes is more instructive than any general precepts of a more philosophical nature could be. He said approvingly of Thucydides:

> Digressions for instruction's cause, and other such open conveyances of precepts (which is the philosopher's part), he never useth; . . . the narration itself doth secretly instruct the reader, and more effectually than can possibly be done by precept.[4]

It would be unwise to read too much into these early remarks, but they do suggest that Hobbes at this time had no serious quarrel with what may be called the inductivist approach to politics recommended by Machiavelli, Bodin and Bacon. Its programme was the extraction, from the study of past actions, of general maxims which the wise politician could apply as occasion offered. Bacon, who called this sort of historical

[1] *EW* vii, p. 468.   [2] *EW* viii, p. vii.   [3] p. xxiv.   [4] p. xxii.

analysis 'ruminated history',[1] spoke approvingly of the form of writing

> which Machiavelli most wisely and aptly chose for government; namely, observations or discourses upon histories and examples. For knowledge drawn freshly . . . out of particulars knows best the way back to particulars again; and it contributes much more to practice . . .[2]

Machiavelli himself had written in *The Prince*:

> The prince ought to read history and study the actions of eminent men, see how they acted in warfare, examine the causes of their victories and defeats in order to imitate the former and avoid the latter.[3]

But in case the prince was too busy, Machiavelli had done the work for him. He explained in his Dedication that he had distilled the political lessons of 'a long experience of modern events and a constant study of the past' into a small volume to enable the prince to learn them 'in a very short time'. Machiavelli justified his inductivist programme by an appeal to the constancy of human nature:

> *He who would forecast what is about to happen should look to what has been*; since all human events, whether present or to come, have their exact counterpart in the past. And this, because these events are brought about by men, whose passions and dispositions remaining in all ages the same, naturally give rise to the same effects.[4]

How much reliance should the prince place on these inductively derived maxims of statecraft? In the penultimate chapter of *The Prince* Machiavelli makes a striking admission. Here, it turns out that a calculating application of them is rather likely to lead to *failure*. A far-reaching, and usually decisive,

---

[1] *De Augmentis Scientiarum* II, x & *Works* iv, p. 310.
[2] VIII, ii, Proverb 34 & *Works* v, p. 56.
[3] *The Prince*, ch. xiv.
[4] *Discourses*, bk. III, ch. xliii, my italics.

role in worldly affairs is played by *Fortune*.[1] For Machiavelli, 'Fortune' is a name, not just for the element of incalculability in human affairs, but for a real agency, feminine, powerful and capricious. To overcome her, not calculation but youthfulness, audacity and impetuosity are wanted.

This admission deprives the earlier chapters of much of their point. Not only are calculated attempts to put their lessons into practice likely to miscarry, but the historical instances from which those lessons were drawn are now suspect: an action or policy may have proved successful, not because of any particular merit in it, but because Fortune smiled on its author; despite its success, it may be a bad example to follow. If Fortune rules half our actions, then even the most exact counterpart today of an action in the past will, as likely as not, have a different outcome.

When Hobbes, who nowhere mentions Machiavelli by name, wrote the *Tract* he was already a full-fledged physical determinist who could hardly take such talk about Fortune literally—could hardly allow that a supernatural agency may interfere with naturally determined events. The great determinist and materialist of antiquity, Democritus, had said: 'Men have fashioned an image of Chance as an excuse for their own stupidity.'[2] A determinist regards all seemingly random or accidental events as determined by factors of which we are more or less ignorant. Thus in the *Tract* Hobbes held a position which implied that anyone who imputes political uncertainty to Fortune is merely confessing his own ignorance. This was stated explicitly in *Leviathan*:

In many occasions they put for cause of natural events their own ignorance; but disguised in other words: as when they say,

---

[1] 'At times I am partly inclined to share this opinion [that *everything* is governed by fortune]. Nevertheless, that our free-will may not be altogether extinguished, I think it may be true that fortune is the ruler of half our actions, but that she allows the other half or thereabouts to be governed by us' (*The Prince*, ch. xxv). 'All who stand in her way, she either removes by death, or deprives of the means of effecting good' (*Discourses*, II, xxix).

[2] Fr. 119 in Kathleen Freeman, *Ancilla to the Pre-Socratic Philosophers*, 1948, p. 104.

Fortune is the cause of things contingent; that is, of things whereof they know no cause.[1]

Machiavelli's idea of the forecastability of 'what is about to happen' in human affairs presupposed, first that general laws can somehow be gathered from history, and second that sufficient knowledge of the circumstances of an action is possible for its success or failure to be predicted with the help of such laws. Hobbes came to reject both these assumptions. He was a determinist who denied the possibility of scientific forecasting. Already in *The Elements of Law* he emphasized the point (usually associated with Hume) that there can be no valid inference from 'Every observed *A* has been *B*' to 'Every *A* is *B*' or to 'The next *A* will be *B*'. Such inductive generalizations and predictions, he says, are essentially 'conjectural': 'their assurance is more or less; but never full and evident . . . Experience concludeth nothing universally.'[2] Laws cannot be gathered from history. And even if we have got them from some other quarter, Hobbes added in *Leviathan* that science cannot deliver unconditional forecasts or, indeed, make any unconditional statements:

> As for the knowledge of consequence, which . . . is called science, it is not absolute, but conditional. No man can know by discourse, that this, or that, is, has been, or will be; which is to know absolutely: but only, that if this be, that is . . . : which is to know conditionally.[3]

An illustration: for Hobbes it was a scientific law that

[1] p. 375 & *EW* iii, p. 679; and see p. 55 & p. 100, *De Corp* II, x, 5 & *EW* i, p. 130, and *EW* vi, p. 216.

[2] I, iv, 10 & *EW* iv, pp. 17–18. There is in *De Corpore* a hint of a further anti-inductivist argument, which might be stated thus: even if we *could* somehow infer 'Every crow is black' from 'Every observed crow has been black', we still could not infer that it is a *law of nature* that crows be black. 'Every crow is black' would be a contingent proposition; and 'in contingent propositions, though this be true, *every crow is black*, yet this, *if any thing be a crow, the same is black*, is false' (I, iii, 11 & *EW* i, p. 39): it might be that a non-black crow *could* be, but never *will* be, bred.

[3] p. 30 & *EW* iii, p. 52.

Whatsoever is moved, will always be moved, except there be some other body beside it, which causeth it to rest. [1]

This tells us that *if* nothing obstructed a moving body, it *would* continue to move indefinitely. But there is an immense difference between this conditional statement and an unconditional (or 'absolute') forecast about a particular body's movements during the next ten minutes. To make such a forecast with certainty one would need to know that one knew all the relevant initial conditions; and *this* one never could know: it would always be *possible* (and often very probable) that one had overlooked a disturbing factor. This applies no less to attempts to forecast the outcome of political actions:

Sometimes a man desires to know the event of an action . . . supposing like events will follow like actions . . . [But] such conjecture, *through the difficulty of observing all circumstances*, be very fallacious. [2]

The forecasts of 'him that has most experience', though the least unreliable, still do not have 'certainty enough'; only God has 'foresight of things to come'. In *Behemoth* Hobbes dismissed as 'madmen' those who pretend to 'foretell future contingencies' (though he allowed that a prophecy may be effective propaganda, 'prophecy being many times the principal cause of the event foretold').[3] In the light of these ideas, Machiavelli's idea of Fortune looks like a conspiracy-theory to excuse the unreliability of his inductivist method.

There was sufficient analogy between inductive reasoning and judicial reasoning as understood by a common lawyer like Sir Edward Coke, to allow Hobbes to extend his critique of the former to the latter. Coke and his followers contended, against James I and Charles I, that in the event of a conflict between a

---

[1] *De Corp* II, viii, 19 & *EW* i, p. 115. 'I agree absolutely with you', Leibniz wrote to Hobbes, 'that one body is not moved by another unless the latter touches it and is in motion and that, once begun, every motion continues unless impeded by something' (*PPL* i, p. 164 & *G* vii, p. 573).

[2] *Lev* p. 10 & *EW* iii, pp. 14–15, my italics.

[3] *EW* vi, pp. 398–9; and see *Lev* p. 226 & *EW* iii, p. 414, where an example of a self-verifying prophecy is cited.

statute law or royal ordinance and the common law, the latter should prevail: the common law is the supreme law. This conflicted, not merely with Hobbes's view about where the sovereignty in England lay (namely with the King), but with his more general conviction that sovereignty must lie with some clearly defined *person* or body of persons (see below, p. 157). He regarded Aristotle's saying that not men should govern, but the laws, as a pernicious error;[1] with the help of this motto common lawyers were contending, in effect, that not the King, but the judges should govern, though without seeming to do so and in a circumscribed way; these common lawyers pretended that a judge, even when he extends the law to a new kind of case, is not a law-*maker* but only *discovers* what the law is, by examining previous judicial decisions and extrapolating from them general principles which extend to the case before him. Since those earlier decisions were made by extrapolating from still earlier decisions . . . no one, on this view, is responsible for the present state of the law of the land and no one may overhaul it: the supreme law has just grown—broadened down from precedent to precedent—and the legislature may only supplement it.[2]

But the quasi-inductivist principle that one can gather from a series of past decisions what the next decision should be was, for Hobbes, no less objectionable than the principle that one can gather from a series of past instances what the next instance will be.

> For though in all places of the world, men should lay the foundation of their houses on the sand, it could not thence be inferred, that so it ought to be.[3]

[1] *Lev* pp. 377–8 & *EW* iii, pp. 683–4.

[2] See Hobbes's *Dialogue . . . of the Common Laws* in *EW* vi. For a common lawyer's reply, see Sir Mathew Hale's 'Reflections on Hobbes's *Dialogue of the Law*' (printed in Sir William Holdsworth's *History of English Law*, v, pp. 500–13).

[3] *Lev* p. 107 & *EW* iii, p. 195. Cp. Lord Eldon: 'Dumpor's case always struck me as extraordinary: but if you depart from Dumpor's case, what is there to prevent a departure in every direction?' (Quoted by W. Bagehot, *Literary Studies*, Everyman, i, p. 10.)

Hobbes answers Coke's claim that judicial reasoning requires 'long study, observation, and experience', with the comment:

> It is possible long study may increase and confirm erroneous sentences: and where men build on false grounds, the more they build, the greater is the ruin: and of those that study, and observe with equal time and diligence, the reasons and resolutions are and must remain discordant.[1]

Discordant conclusions are to be expected when different men make non-logical inferences from a welter of inappropriate premises.

So much for what Hobbes turned against, after *Thucydides*. Now let us see what he was turning to.

§ 7   *The* Tract

Strauss quoted approvingly[2] Robertson's statement (given on p. 27 above) that Hobbes's political doctrine 'doubtless had its main lines fixed when he was still a mere observer of men and manners'. Now it appears that Robertson's book was already written when he learnt of the *Tract*; for in a footnote, presumably added in proof, he said: 'the complexion of the case is somewhat altered by a tract to which Herr F. Tönnies has first called attention'.[3]

Strauss set the *Tract* aside as 'of no great interest for our purpose'.[4] It seems to me, on the contrary, of disturbing interest to someone who upholds the priority and independence of Hobbes's central political ideas; for it is a first sketch of Hobbes's theory, not just of the physical world, but of the world *and of man's natural situation in it*; and in Section III, which briefly depicts man's natural situation, Hobbes states for the first time several ideas which afterwards played a key role in his as yet unformulated political philosophy.

The large problem tackled in the *Tract* is: How are we able

---

[1] *Lev* p. 140 & *EW* iii, p. 256.
[2] *The Political Philosophy of Hobbes*, p. xiii.
[3] *Hobbes*, p. 35 n.   [4] p. xvi.

to see distant bodies like the sun and the stars? Unlike, say, the problem of the tides, which requires only physical theories for its solution, this problem demands not only physical theories about the source and transmission of light, but also a theory about what happens at the receiving end. It demands consideration of stars, medium, and observers in a single system. At about the time when Hobbes most probably wrote the *Tract*, Descartes wrote a work entitled *Le Monde*;[1] this was sub-titled *ou Traité de la Lumière*, because he believed that most cosmological problems are contained in the problem of light:

> Fearing that I could not put in my Treatise all that I had in my mind, I undertook only to show very fully my conceptions of light . . . Light proceeds almost entirely from [the sun and fixed stars]; the heavens would be dealt with because they transmit light, the planets, the comets and the earth because they reflect it . . .; and finally I should deal with man because he is the spectator of all.[2]

The problem of light started both Descartes and Hobbes on the construction of a cosmological theory which would comprehend the human observer and his interaction with the external world.[3]

The style of the *Tract*, quite unlike that of *Thucydides*, is modelled on Euclid. Section I lays down certain general mechanistic principles. Section II extends these to action at a distance and illumination. Section III gives a causal account of

[1] He decided not to publish it when he heard of the Inquisition's condemnation of Galileo.

[2] *Discourse* Pt v & *PW* i, p. 107.

[3] Raymond Polin sees this contrast between the two men: Descartes 'compose une philosophie de l'univers où l'homme trouve sa place, [Hobbes] écrit une philosophie de l'homme, qu'il prendra pour modèle lorsqu'il esquissera une philosophie de l'univers. [Descartes] est d'abord un géomètre, un physicien, [Hobbes] d'abord un humaniste et un moraliste' (*Politique et Philosophie chez Hobbes*, 1953, p. xiii). Yet their cosmologies were almost identical; and Hobbes's mechanistic principles invade the human sphere more completely than do those of Descartes, who reserved for man free-will and an immaterial soul, and whose laws of motion allow for the voluntary redirection of physical processes.

the production of visual images ('phantasma') in the brain of the observer as a result of external pressures on his nervous system ('animal spirits'). One might have expected Hobbes to stop here, now that his outline account of how we perceive distant bodies was complete. Instead, he proceeds from 'the act of sense' to 'the act of understanding', and thence to 'the act of appetite', and finally to the meaning of *good* and *bad*. The *Tract* is a condensed, preliminary statement of Hobbes's cosmology, psychology and ethics. With one exception, its ideas survived, essentially unaltered, into his later philosophical and political writings.

The exception has some interest and may be dealt with at once. In Section II Hobbes begins by laying down the principle that one body can act on another at a distance from it in one of two ways only: either it imparts to the surrounding physical medium a movement which is transmitted to the other body, or it throws out particles ('species') from itself, some of which hit the other body (emission-theory). Next, Hobbes proceeds, by an argument which need not detain us, to the conclusion that if a luminous body transmitted light in the first way, it could happen that a shaded surface was brighter than an exposed surface. This being contrary to experience, luminous bodies must transmit light in the second way.

But Hobbes afterwards repudiated the emission-theory (which goes back to the Greek atomists, who spoke of 'effluences' being thrown off the surfaces of things, flying through the void, and striking the observer's eye).[1] And it is not difficult to see why. Already in the *Tract* he mentioned one difficulty: 'If bodyes continually send out so many substantiall species, how can they subsist without supply? This indeed is hard to determine.'[2] Besides this replenishment problem, there is the graver objection that if a luminous body is forever hurling out of itself, in all directions, particles travelling at immense speed for immense distances, it must surely have some

[1] For an account of the objections raised in antiquity to this theory, see Cyril Bailey, *The Greek Atomists and Epicurus*, 1928, pp. 165 f.

[2] Sect. ii, conc. 8.

inherent power of self-movement. But the impossibility of self-movement was already a central, and explicit, idea of the *Tract*. It was implied by the mechanistic metaphysics propounded there; and Hobbes added the following *reductio ad absurdum* argument to clinch the matter: suppose that a body on which no external force is acting *does* have the power to move itself; *ex hypothesi* there is nothing outside it to determine *when* and in *what direction* it moves itself; hence it moves itself always and in all directions, which is impossible.[1]

The first two sentences of the *Tract* announce what proved to be the permanent core of Hobbes's cosmology:

1. That, whereto nothing is added, and from which nothing is taken, remains in the same state it was.
2. That which is in no way *touch'd* [my italics] by another, hath nothing added to nor taken from it.

We may summarize this in the motto, *No change without push.* As we saw (p. 21), this doctrine is (in our sense) metaphysical: observed change may be caused by pressure from bodies which are insensibly small or otherwise unobservable. But although empirically irrefutable, it has important implications, especially for the philosophy of mind. It leads straight to determinism and the denial of free-will. If every change is the result of physical pressure, every change is externally caused; and if every change is externally caused, every human decision is externally caused. In the *Tract* Hobbes says that the concept of a free agent as one which, all things requisite to work being given, may or may not work, is self-contradictory.[2]

No change without push implies that psychological happenings must be changes in something *material*. A thought, or a

[1] Sect. i, conc. 10. This argument reappeared in *De Corp* II, viii, 19 & *EW* i, p. 115; and see *EW* vii, p. 85. It was subsequently criticized by Hume, on the ground that it assumes the very point at issue, namely that there *must* be an external cause of [the time and direction of] motion (*Treatise* I, iii, 3, & p. 80); but if we may conceive a body to move itself without external cause, then we may further conceive it to move itself at a particular time and in a certain direction without external cause.

[2] Sect. i, conc. 11.

feeling, need not itself be regarded as a material thing (the *flight* of a cannon-ball is not a thing) but it must not be regarded as an immaterial thing; it should be regarded as a changing condition of a material thing, for it is only material things that can have changes caused in them by other things pressing on them. Thinking and feeling must be regarded as activities which bodies of some kinds are prodded into. At this point we may, for a moment, look ahead from the *Tract* to Hobbes's main objection to Descartes' *Meditations*. Descartes had concluded from the only truth of which he could be absolutely sure—namely, that he thinks and therefore exists —that he is therefore 'a thing which thinks, that is to say, a mind or a soul, or an understanding, or a reason'.[1] Hobbes pounced on this inference: 'it does not seem to be good reasoning to say: I am exercising thought, *hence* I am thought' —any more than it would be to say: I am walking, hence I am *walking-substance*.[2] If such inferences were valid there would be as many substances as there are activities. (We should have to say that a dog barks because it is a barking substance.) In fact, Hobbes insisted, 'the subjects of all activities can be conceived only after a corporeal fashion'[3]—one simply cannot imagine an immaterial *je ne sais quoi* carrying on some activity.

In the *Tract* the *No change without push* doctrine leads naturally to a sensationalist psychology: a man's conceptions of external things result from pressures on his sense-organs, from 'the severall actions of externall things upon the animal spirits, by severall organs'.[4] Any kind of mental spontaneity— free choice, invention of ideas—is impossible.

Just as *No change without push* implies that all pulling is really some kind of pushing (a typical 'haunted-universe' doctrine) so it implies that all so-called final causes are really some sort of efficient cause in disguise: it seems 'as if we draw

---

[1] *Meditation* II & *PW* i, p. 152.

[2] See *PW* ii, p. 61. I have tried to render Hobbes's phrase, 'sum ambulans, *ergo* sum ambulatio', in a way which brings out the point of his objection.

[3] *PW* ii, p. 62.   [4] Sect. iii, conc. 3.

the object to us, whereas the object rather drawes us to it by locall motion'.[1] Hobbes's account leads to a remarkable inversion of the traditional idea of agent and patient: if I reach out for a glass of beer, *it* is the agent and I am the patient.

> The act of appetite is a motion of the animal spirits towards the object that moveth them.
> The *object* is the efficient cause, or *agent* . . .
> *Appetite* . . . is a *passive* power . . . to be moved toward the object . . .[2]

The only candidates available to be called *good* in a world where organisms have no choice but to go after objects which causally attract them are those very objects:

> Good is to every thing, that which hath active power to attract it locally.[3]

By corollary, bad is to every thing that which has active power to repel it. Hobbes adds:

> that which is desirable or good to one, may not be so to another, . . . what attracts one, may not attract another.

From this follows an important point in Hobbes's subsequent account of men's natural condition, namely that by nature there are no common standards of good and bad (so that, if common standards are to exist, they must first be *created*).

Another destructive implication may be stated in the words of Ralph Cudworth (Cudworth was attacking Hobbes's full-fledged world-view; but what he says applies to the fledgeling version of it in the *Tract*):

> The upshot . . . is, that there is no such scale or ladder in nature . . ., no degrees of real perfection . . . one above another, as of life

[1] Sect. iii, conc. 7.

[2] Sect. iii, conc. 8. As Brandt says: 'Hobbes's exposition was remarkable [for] the fact that neither the soul, the brain, the will nor the appetite contain any original principle of motion. . . . All motion in the animal spirits originates from without' (*Thomas Hobbes' Mechanical Conception of Nature*, p. 38.)

[3] Sect. iii, conc. 7.

and sense above inanimate matter, of reason and understanding above sense . . . The whole universe is . . . flat and level, . . . nothing but the same uniform matter . . . variegated by diversity of accidental modifications . . .[1]

The classical idea of a naturally ordered, hierarchical world-system[2] depended essentially on the belief that what exists at one level is not the product of what exists at lower levels—that matter cannot give rise to life and appetite, or brutish experience to rational understanding. But the *Tract* is an essay in what may be called ontological reductionism: understanding is reduced to complex experience, evaluation to appetite, and experience and appetite to complex varieties of externally stimulated motion.

Associated with the idea that the world is a natural hierarchy was the Aristotelian-Thomist idea that there is a natural hierarchy among mankind. If the *Tract* does not, by implication, actually contradict this, it does at least imply that any natural gradations among men will be due to merely quantitative differences. (An important addition which Hobbes made later was that such quantitative differences are never large enough to put one man securely above the rest; see below, p. 117.) For men, according to the picture of them given in the *Tract*, are made of the same stuff and activated in the same sort of way. Strauss held that it was only in *Leviathan* that Hobbes's scientism finally forced him to discard his original belief in a certain 'aristocratic virtue'.[3] But already in *The Elements of Law* Hobbes had written:

> The question, which is the better man, is determinable only in the estate of government and policy, though it be mistaken for a question of nature, not only by ignorant men, that think one man's blood better than another's by nature; but also by [Aristotle].[4]

And this was entirely in line with the *Tract*.

---

[1] *TIS* iv, pp. 125–7. (I have severely pruned a rather prolix statement.)
[2] For a history of this idea, see A. O. Lovejoy, *The Great Chain of Being*, 1936.
[3] *The Political Philosophy of Hobbes*, p. 55.
[4] I, xvii, 1 & *EW* iv, p. 102.

III

Scientific Tradition

In this chapter enough of the prehistory of Hobbes's method will be sketched to explain why Hobbes preferred a traditional method to either of the new methods of Bacon and Descartes. We shall lose sight of Hobbes himself for a time, but our efforts will not have been misspent: we shall get a preview of the main ideas which went into his method, whose large political significance will be the subject of the next chapter.

§ 8   *Methodological situation*

It was generally agreed among more advanced thinkers of the first half of the seventeenth century that, although men are equipped by nature to find out the truth about the world, contemporary science was still only in its infancy. They agreed, further, that this backwardness was largely the result of a timid dependence on past 'authorities' (especially Aristotle). But this could not be the whole explanation. For men cannot *always* have been in thrall to still earlier 'authorities'—Adam had no Aristotle to cling to, and Aristotle himself, it was generally agreed, did not rely on others but examined things independently.[1] If Adam was naturally equipped to discover

---

[1] 'It is the followers of Aristotle who have crowned him with authority, not he who has usurped or appropriated it to himself' (Galileo, *TCWS*, p. 111).

'I find not that the ancients they cite, took it for an ornament to do the like with those that wrote before them' (Hobbes, *Lev* p. 395 & *EW* iii, p. 712).

the truth[1] why did his descendants make so little progress that eventually they gave up, preferring to pretend that the main work had already been done? The standard answer was that although men have the right tools, they lack the untutored ability to use them effectively; nature, so to speak, gives each of us a do-it-yourself kit, but omits instructions for its use.

This answer ushered in the age of method: nature's omission must be made good; the right method of employing our faculties must be discovered. Until this is done, men will go on fumbling ineffectively. 'Neither the naked hand nor the understanding left to itself can effect much', Bacon wrote. 'It is by instruments and helps that the work is done, which are as much wanted for the understanding as for the hand.'[2] Descartes insisted that the right method is indispensable if the fundamental truths about the world which are innate in all men are to be brought to light: 'it were far better never to think of investigating truth at all, than to do so without a method'.[3] And Hobbes, in the opening paragraph of *De Corpore*, wrote:

> Every man brought Philosophy, that is, Natural Reason, into the world with him; for all men can reason to some degree, and concerning some things: but . . . most men wander out of the way, and *fall into error for want of method.*[4]

If the idea of the indispensability of method explains why primitive men made no scientific progress, it at the same time creates an awkward new problem: if no important discovery can be made without the right method, how can the right method itself be discovered? For this would be the most important discovery of all.

Bacon claimed in the 'Epistle Dedicatory' to the *Novum Organum* that he had discovered the right method ('I have provided the machine') thanks to a God-given accident. The things in his work being 'totally new in their very kind', it is

---

[1] 'A man may be a philosopher alone by himself, without any master; Adam had this capacity' (Hobbes, *De Corp* I, vi, 11 & *EW* i, p. 80).

[2] *Novum Organum* Part I, aph. 2 & *Works* iv, p. 47.

[3] *Rules for the Direction of the Mind*, Rule iv & *PW* i, p. 9.

[4] *EW* i, p. 1, my italics.

indeed a 'wonder' that they 'should have come into any man's mind'—'no doubt there is something of accident' about it; 'this accident . . . may be ascribed to the infinite mercy and goodness of God'.[1]

Descartes likewise regarded *his* discovery of the true method as a happy accident. He said in the *Discourse*:

> I have had *great good fortune* from my youth up, in *lighting upon* and pursuing certain paths which have conducted me to considerations and maxims from which I have formed a *Method*.[2]

Thus each of these men claimed, in effect, that the human condition had recently undergone a dramatic transformation: before, men had struggled along without a method, getting nowhere; then came the *annus mirabilis* and the method was known. Men now, for the first time, had it in their power to attain true knowledge of the world. Their first step should obviously be to sweep away the rubbish accumulated during the pre-method era.

> There remains but one course for the recovery of a sound and healthy condition,—namely, that *the entire work of the understanding be commenced afresh*, and the mind itself be from the very outset not left to take its own course, but guided at every step; and the business be done as if by machinery.[3]

It was possible, however, for those who broadly agreed with Bacon and Descartes about the need for a method, to take a very different view of its creation. Instead of a one-man once-and-for-all invention, they could regard it as the outcome of a step-by-step development, at the beginning of which a very rudimentary method had been used to create, among other things, a less crude method which had in turn been used to create a better one, and so on.[4] This view has large advantages

---

[1] *Works* iv, pp. 11–12. [2] *PW* i, p. 82, my italics.

[3] F. Bacon, *Novum Organum*, Pref. & *Works* iv, p. 40, my italics.

[4] Spinoza afterwards gave a very clear statement of this view: 'In order to discover the best method for finding out the truth, there is no need of another method to discover such method; nor of a third method for discovering the second, and so on to infinity. . . . The matter stands on the

over the Bacon-Descartes view. It does not have to make a self-indulgent exception to the claim that discoveries are impossible without a method. It does not credit one man with the chance discovery of the philosopher's stone. And it does not have the damning implications for all scientific work done before the alleged *annus mirabilis*: if the method of science has been gradually developed, good scientific work may have been done before it was quite perfected.

Hobbes agreed that a huge amount of intellectual rubbish had been accumulated, especially in the ancient universities. But the decisive point is that he believed that *some* genuine science already existed. The sciences which now exist are all young, he said, but they have already advanced far. He acknowledged Gilbert's work,[1] and credited Copernicus with the founding of astronomy, since 'extraordinarily advanced' by Kepler; and he gave the highest praise to Galileo and Harvey:

> Galileus in our time . . . was the first that opened to us the gate of natural philosophy universal, which is the knowledge of the nature of *motion* . . . Lastly, the science of *man's body*, the most profitable part of natural science, was first discovered with admirable sagacity by our countryman Doctor Harvey.[2]

He could not accept a methodological doctrine which implied that all this work was no good. If 'men wander out of the way, and fall into error for want of method', then men like Galileo and Harvey, who have obviously found the way, must already

---

same footing as the making of material tools. . . . Men at first made use of the instruments supplied by nature to accomplish very easy pieces of workmanship, laboriously and imperfectly, and then, when these were finished, wrought other things more difficult. . . . So, in like manner, the intellect, by its native strength, makes for itself intellectual instruments, whereby it acquires strength for performing other intellectual operations and from these operations gets again fresh instruments, or the power of pushing its investigations further, and thus gradually proceeds till it reaches the summit of wisdom' (*Works*, tr. Elwes, ii, pp. 11–12).

[1] *EW* vii, p. 57.

[2] *De Corp* Ep. Ded. & *EW* i, p. viii. Descartes' name is conspicuous by its absence; see below, p. 122.

possess a pretty powerful method. What was now needed was not a fresh start under the aegis of a new method, but the extension of their method to new fields.

Hobbes regarded himself as the first to extend it to politics. His *De Cive* opens with an informal account of it (see pp. 71–2 below); and the passage just quoted, in which he salutes Galileo and Harvey, continues:

> Natural Philosophy is therefore but young; but Civil Philosophy is yet much younger, as being no older (I say it provoked, and that my detractors may know how little they have wrought upon me) than my own book *De Cive*.

In *Leviathan* he said that men have hitherto lacked the method for finding out the scientific rules for making and maintaining commonwealths.[1] He saw himself as the junior member of a little band of scientific pioneers; and these pioneers belonged to a common methodological tradition.

Harvey and Hobbes were friends;[2] they were equally unimpressed by the inductivist philosophy of Bacon, whose secretary Hobbes had once been and whose physician Harvey became.[3] Hobbes did not meet Galileo until 1635–6, when Hobbes was staying in Florence.[4] But Harvey had studied at the University of Padua during 1598–1602, when Galileo was a professor there. At Padua, during the sixteenth century, a conception of scientific method had been worked out which Galileo and Harvey, and afterwards Hobbes, adopted. We will now investigate this for its bearing on Hobbes's civil philosophy.

[1] p. 107 & *EW* iii, pp. 195–6.

[2] In a codicil to his will Harvey left £10 'to my good friend Mr. Tho Hobbs to buy something to keepe in remembrance of me' (*Works*, p. xciv). For Hobbes's respectful and sympathetic feelings for 'that most civil and renowned old man Dr. Harvey', see *EW* vii, p. 338.

[3] Harvey derisively remarked to Aubrey that Bacon 'writes philosophy like a Lord Chancelor' (*Brief Lives*, ed. A. Clark, i, p. 299).

[4] See J. J. Fahie, *Galileo: his life and work*, 1903, p. 390.

§ 9   *Paduan methodology*[1]

The intuitive idea which informs this methodological tradition was this: the way to understand something is to take it apart, in deed or in thought, ascertain the nature of its parts, and then reassemble it—resolve it and recompose it. Already in the fourteenth century Pietro d'Abano had spoken (in connection with medical science) of 'the way of resolution' and 'the way of composition':

> The way of composition . . . is the contrary of the first way. In it you begin with the thing at which you have arrived by the way of resolution, and then return to the very things resolved, and put them together again in their proper order.[2]

Behind this was the further idea that things may be broken up until the *simplest elements* are reached and the *first principles* governing them are ascertained. This idea had been stated at the beginning of Aristotle's *Physics*:

> We do not think that we know a thing until we are acquainted with its . . . first principles, and have carried our analysis as far as its simplest elements . . . The natural way of doing this is to start from the things which are more knowable and obvious to us and proceed towards those which are clearer and more knowable by nature.

What comes first in the order of our knowledge is the medium-sized complexes, exhibiting surface-regularities, with which we are acquainted in a rough, empirical way. But in the order of nature these are end-products, formed from simple elements governed by first principles. These latter, first in the order of nature, are last in the order of discovery. To understand something scientifically we have to resolve or analyse it into these ultimate causes, and then, their nature ascertained, recompose it by tracing deductively their production of it. There is 'a double procedure in natural science'[3]—a resolutive method followed by a compositive method.

[1] I shall mainly rely upon the excellent quotations in J. H. Randall Jr.'s *The School of Padua*, Padova, 1961.

[2] Quoted by Randall, p. 31.   [3] Paul of Venice, quoted by Randall, p. 40.

The end of the resolutive method is discovery. . . . In the performance of its functions [this method] is exceedingly efficacious; and we employ it for the discovery of those things that are very obscure and hidden.[1]

But did the Paduan methodologists really regard their method as a discovery-making procedure whose systematic application would make nature reveal her secrets one after another? Randall interprets them as doing so.[2] But the evidence he provides will hardly sustain this interpretation. Of Agostino Nifo, Randall comments:

The method by which principles are arrived at is . . . the guarantee of their validity. . . . Nifo has merely made explicit what is implicit in the long previous discussion.[3]

But this hardly fits Randall's own quotations, in the course of which Nifo says:

. . . the first process, by which the discovery of the cause is put into syllogistic form, is a mere hypothetical (*coniecturalis*) syllogism . . . That something is a cause can never be so certain as that an effect exists; for the existence of an effect is known to the senses. That it is the cause remains conjectural. . . .[4]

In view of this, Nifo could hardly have regarded it as a method which *guarantees the validity* of those principles arrived at with its help.

Admittedly, Zabarella (whose methodological writings Randall regards as the consummation of Paduan methodology) often writes as if the resolutive method were a foolproof

[1] Zabarella, quoted by Randall, pp. 52–3. To modern ears, this sounds rather too good to be true. The very *progress* of science has led us to give up the belief in the ascertainability of simplest elements and first principles; we now rather expect that each new candidate for the role of simple element will afterwards turn out to be complex, and that each new candidate for the role of first principle will afterwards be subordinated to superior principles.

[2] *Ibid.*, p. 49; see also pp. 16, 26, 55–6 and 107.

[3] *Ibid.*, p. 47. [4] Quoted *ibid.*, pp. 44–5.

instrument for making scientific discoveries. In *De Natura Logicae* he speaks of 'instruments by which in all things the true may be known and distinguished from the false'; and in *De Methodis* he writes:

> Method is an intellectual instrument producing knowledge of the unknown from the known. . . . Method has the force of inference, and concludes this from that.[1]

> Resolutive method is a syllogism consisting of necessary propositions which leads from things that are posterior and effects that are better known to the discovery of prior things and causes.[2]

However, this confident tone is absent in his *De Regressu*. There he talks of 'hitting upon' the cause[3] (but one does not *hit upon* the conclusion of a syllogism), and says that it is only 'gradually' that we are led to the cause of an effect (but one is not led *gradually* to infer the conclusion of a syllogism). And he concedes that *hypotheses* are indispensable: 'where we form no hypothesis at all, we shall never discover anything'. It is as if Zabarella came to realize that his earlier claim that the resolutive method is an 'exceedingly efficacious' instrument 'for the discovery of those things that are very obscure and hidden' had been rather too sanguine.

He had good reason for modifying his original claim; for members of this school had gone out of their way to emphasize the *disparities* between an observed effect and its hidden causes: the effect may appear to be simple and homogeneous, for example, although its internal constitution is complex. (A striking example of this came later with Newton's discovery that apparently 'homogeneal' sunlight is really 'heterogeneal'.) Moreover, the same effect may be produced in different ways. In *The Assayer*, Galileo (whom Randall regards as the supreme practitioner of the Paduan method) tells a charming story of a lonely countryman who believed that musical notes were produced only by birds. In time he learned that they were also

---

[1] Quoted *ibid*, p. 50.   [2] Quoted *ibid*., p. 51.
[3] Quoted *ibid*., p. 58; for Galileo's similar phrase, see *TCWS*, p. 51.

produced by flutes, and violins, and organs, and in many other unexpected ways. The story was to illustrate 'Nature's bounty and variety of methods for producing her effects'.[1] But all this means that we cannot, as Zabarella had originally claimed, make syllogistic or any other kind of logical inferences from a description of an effect to an account of its causes. These may be got at only by conjectures. It seems that Nifo saw this and that Zabarella came near to seeing it.

That the resolutive method is no instrument of discovery does not mean that it is without implications for the conduct of scientific enquiries. Moreover, it is particularly suggestive for *social* enquiries. In the physical domain it is usually medium-sized wholes which are, in Aristotle's phrase, 'more knowable and obvious to us', and their elements, and the principles which govern these, which are remote from ordinary experience. But in the social domain it is the elements (i.e. people) that are more knowable and obvious, and the 'wholes' (i.e. social institutions) that are more of less theoretical. Thus the methodological prescription 'Resolve wholes into their elements' has a more definite purport for the political philosopher than it has for the natural philosopher, whose hardest problem is usually to guess *what* the elements are.

§ 10 Galileo

Galileo's investigation of the trajectories of projectiles may be represented as a beautiful exemplification of Paduan method. Initially, he is confronted by some rough empirical facts: 'it has been observed that missiles and projectiles describe a curved path of some sort';[2] and 'from accounts given by gunners' he already knows that cannon and mortars have a maximum range at an elevation of $45°$.[3]

Before the main analysis begins, he simplifies the problem

---

[1] See *DO*, pp. 256–8. Descartes pointed out that even a straight line— 'the simplest of all'—may be the resultant of infinitely diverse movements (*Principes de la Philosophie* II, § 32).

[2] *TNS*, p. 153.   [3] p. 276.

by disengaging it from certain empirical complications: for the time being it will be supposed that there is no air resistance or other friction, and no curvature of the earth. (This does not mean that the results of the subsequent analysis will apply only to ideal projectiles; these complicating factors can be reintroduced afterwards.)

At the beginning of the 'Fourth Day' Galileo takes the relatively simple case of a heavy projectile gliding along, and then passing over the edge of, a raised horizontal plane. He resolves its subsequent path into a horizontal motion and a downward motion. During the 'Third Day' it had been established that 'any velocity once imparted to a moving body will be rigidly maintained as long as the external causes of acceleration or retardation are removed, a condition which is found only on horizontal planes';[1] and also that a freely falling body acquires equal increments of speed during equal time-intervals. Hence our projectile will have both these motions, the geometrical resultant of which is a semi-parabola. From here, Galileo proceeds to an array of new results, including an explanation of a cannon's having a maximum range at an elevation of 45° and the prediction of 'what has perhaps never been observed in experience, namely, that of other shots those which exceed or fall short of 45° by equal amounts have equal ranges'.[2] Range-tables are worked out, and the variable factor of air resistance is readmitted.

Seen in this way, the methodological maxim of this scientific achievement is: resolve, idealize, recompose! Hobbes's civil philosophy also exemplifies this maxim.

What, for Galileo, was the epistemological status of his principles? This question is worth answering because—or so I shall claim—there is a striking analogy between his appraisal of his physical principles and Hobbes's appraisal of the principles of his civil philosophy. But it is not a question which allows a quick and confident answer. Although Galileo was one of the most philosophically sophisticated of the great natural scientists, he never vouchsafed a systematic account of

[1] *TNS*, p. 215.   [2] p. 276.

his philosophy of science. The explanation of this seems clear: his situation obliged him to be wary. But he left enough clues scattered about his books for us to be able to reconstruct his theory of knowledge, at least in outline and provided we remember the situation he was in.

His situation was this. The Copernican system, taken literally, conflicted with certain Biblical passages, taken literally. Had some proof of the truth of the Copernican system been forthcoming, the Church would have reluctantly conceded that those Biblical passages should not be taken literally. But no such proof was forthcoming. And in 1616 the Church had officially decided that it was the Copernican system which must not be taken literally, but only as a 'mathematical hypothesis' for making astronomical predictions. Within the Church it was generally assumed that this was Copernicus's own view of his system. The preface to his *De Revolutionibus* stated that the astronomer cannot 'attain to the true causes' of celestial motions and must be content to devise 'such hypotheses as, being assumed, enable the motions to be calculated correctly'. The preface went on to say that 'these hypotheses need not be true, nor even like the truth [*verisimiles*]'.[1] (Later, Kepler revealed that this preface was the unauthorized addition of a certain Osiander, who was seeing the book through the press, and that it completely misrepresented the intention of the dying Copernicus.)[2]

In 1623 Galileo's friend and admirer, Cardinal Barberini, became Pope Urban VIII; and in the following year he granted a number of long and flattering audiences to Galileo, who wanted permission to argue for Copernicanism. It seems that the Pope gave Galileo permission to discuss the Copernican

[1] 'Verisimiles' is usually translated as 'probable'; I have followed K. R. Popper's more literal translation; see his *Conjectures and Refutations*, 1963, p. 98.

[2] The story has been told with his customary skill by A. Koestler: *The Sleepwalkers*, 1959, pp. 165–72; the full text of Osiander's preface is given on pp. 564–6. And see G. de Santillana, *The Crime of Galileo*, 1955, p. 101; and E. Rosen, *3 Copernican Treatises*, 1959, p. 24, n. 68.

system, provided that he emphasized that it was an unverified hypothesis, and that the phenomena it 'saves' may very well be produced by the almighty Author of Nature in some other way.[1] After this Galileo began writing his *Dialogue Concerning Two Chief World Systems*, which was published in 1632. When Urban read it he was furious, and ordered the Inquisition to begin proceedings against Galileo.

Why did Urban round on Galileo? There were probably several reasons.[2] My guess is that one reason was that Urban had not appreciated what a big difference may open out between a so-called 'mathematical hypothesis', which is not regarded as either true or false, and a hypothesis which is true or false but unverifiable. For although the latter can never be *known* to be true, it may *be* true; moreover, it may be argued for so persuasively that it seems very likely to be true. In this *Dialogue* Galileo creates the impression that the choice is between only the 'two great systems'—the Ptolemaic system and the Copernican system. Hence his demolition of the former looks like a complete vindication of the latter. Urban had supposed that, regarded as a useful but unverifiable hypothesis, Copernicanism would not be taken over-seriously. He found that Galileo, without claiming that it was verified, had argued for its truth so effectively that it would be taken very seriously indeed.

At the final hearing of his trial, Galileo was questioned, 'under threat of torture', as to his real conviction concerning the two systems. Instead of resurrecting his pathetic reply, which the Inquisition accepted, let us consider how he might have replied if he could have spoken freely.

In the *Dialogue* he was careful never to claim that the

[1] See Karl von Gebler, *Galileo Galilei and the Roman Curia*, London, 1879, ch. x, and Santillana, *op. cit.*, pp. 160–8.

[2] The old explanation was that it was because the Pope regarded Simplicio—the spokesman for the Ptolemaic system—as a malicious representation of himself (see, e.g., J. J. Fahie, *Galileo*, 1903, p. 268). J. Agassi suggests that it was because 'of the enthusiastic reception of the book' that 'the Pope decided to proceed against Galileo at once' (*Brit. Jour. Phil. Science*, November 1957, p. 239).

Copernican system had been verified. At one point, his spokesman, Salviati, says that he has only advanced certain reasons

> which render it not entirely improbable that the daily rotation
> belongs to the earth rather than to the rest of the universe. Nor do
> I set these forth to you as inviolable laws, but merely as plausible
> reasons. For I understand very well that one single experiment or
> conclusive proof to the contrary would suffice to overthrow
> [them].[1]

And there is one consideration which suggests that Galileo
really did regard the Copernican system as an unverifiable
hypothesis, namely, his insistence (see pp. 54–5 above) on the
unrestricted variety of methods by which nature can produce
her observed effects. This implies that, however successfully the
astronomer may depict *a* way, he can never know that this is
the way, in which the effect is produced.[2] But there is a difference between nature's *mechanisms* and the *natural principles*,
or laws, which govern their workings. Perhaps Galileo only
meant that there is an indefinite number of physically possible
ways of producing a given effect *all in accordance with the same
fixed physical principles*. (Descartes, who regarded his physical
principles as true, added that 'the power of nature is so ample
and so vast, and these principles are so simple and general, that'
almost 'any particular effect . . . might be deduced from the
principles in many different ways'.)[3]

Although Galileo may not have regarded the principles of
Copernicanism as verified, it seems likely that he regarded
them as verif*iable*. For in a note which he added to his own
copy of the *Dialogue* he says that a time may come when 'it
might be physically or logically *proved* that the earth moves
and the sun stands still'.[4] The physical proof to which Galileo
looked forward was the appearance of stellar parallax—

[1] *TCWS*, p. 122.

[2] Thus Galileo says: 'I have never boasted that I could [determine
precisely the way in which comets are produced], knowing that they may
originate in some manner that is far beyond our power of imagination'
(*DO*, p. 258).

[3] *PW* i, p. 121.   [4] *TCWS*, p. v, my italics.

something which obstinately failed to materialize during his lifetime and, indeed, for two centuries afterwards.

Galileo's mention of a possibility of logical proof hints that he hoped that the Copernican system might attain a status even more assured than that of an empirically verified hypothesis.

After his condemnation by the Inquisition, Galileo composed his last and greatest work, *Dialogues Concerning Two New Sciences*. In this book, which does not handle dangerous astronomical issues, Galileo is less reticent in his epistemological appraisal of his main principles. A new epistemological assurance shines through. Near the outset, Salviati proudly announces:

> I wish to convince you by demonstrative reasoning rather than to persuade you by mere probabilities. [1]

Demonstrative science, he says,

> springs from and grows out of principles well-known, understood and conceded by all. [2]

But how, according to Galileo, do these principles come to be well known? Partly, no doubt, by experimental verification. In mechanics and other mathematical sciences

> the principles, once established by well-chosen experiments, become the foundations of the entire superstructure. [3]

But Galileo seems to have believed that there is more to it than experimental verification. After saying that he believes he has depicted the true principle of naturally accelerated motion, Galileo first comments:

> In this belief we are confirmed mainly by the consideration that experimental results are seen to agree with and exactly correspond with those properties which have been, one after another, demonstrated by us. [4]

But, he significantly adds, in this investigation he has been 'led, by hand as it were, in following the habit and custom of

[1] *TNS*, p. 6. [2] p. 87. [3] p. 178. [4] p. 160.

nature . . .' Later, I shall quote passages which suggest that he regarded his scientific principles, not merely as contingent hypotheses which happen to have turned out to be true, but as necessary truths whose truth may come to be seen intuitively. But before we consider this evidence,[1] let us consider what theory of knowledge would enable Galileo to regard his scientific principles both as experimentally verified and, furthermore, as self-evident truths.

One famous theory of knowledge which would do so is Plato's. Briefly, Plato claimed that the soul, before it enters the body, is directly acquainted with the Forms after which the world is modelled. When it enters the body, all this calm knowledge is drowned in the flood of new sensations. But, although it is all forgotten, it is not destroyed. Later, experience of things modelled after a certain Form may jog one into recollecting one's prior knowledge of the Form itself. Experience, on this view, is indispensable for arriving at knowledge which transcends experience.

Galileo does not say that the soul existed before the body. But he does say that human reason is pre-attuned to nature:

> Nature first made things in her own way, and then made human reason skillful enough to be able to understand, but only by hard work, some part of her secrets.[2]

By 'hard work', I take it, Galileo meant the whole difficult business of framing fruitful and exact hypotheses, mathematically deriving testable conclusions from them, devising well-chosen experiments to test them, and observing closely the results of the experiments.

It is entirely consistent with Plato's epistemology that an idea which at first seemed far from self-evident or even downright counter-intuitive should later be seen to be true. One's dormant knowledge of it may be slow to awaken. Galileo often claims that the counter-intuitiveness of truths at which one is at first inclined to boggle may melt away in the course of a scientific examination, so that they 'drop the cloak which has

[1] Bits of which are already to be found in *TCWS*. [2] *TCWS*, p. 265.

hidden them and stand forth in naked and simple beauty'.[1]
After one of Salviati's demonstrations, Sagredo (one of the
other interlocutors) remarks: 'The demonstration is short and
clear; while the proposition which, at first glance, appeared
improbable is now seen to be both true and inevitable.'[2]
Mathematical reasoning combined with well-chosen experiments may, it seems, do more than dispel the air of improba-
bility initially surrounding a scientific proposition, and establish it empirically: such 'hard work' may, in addition, awaken
our inborn but hitherto dormant awareness of the truth of the
proposition.

Plato's theory implies that a teacher cannot lead a pupil to
knowledge of a general truth by trying to instil it into him. His
role should rather be that of an intellectual midwife who helps
his pupils to bring their latent knowledge into consciousness.
His role is to draw things out (as Socrates was supposed to
have done), rather than to stuff things in.

Galileo endorsed this. At one point Sagredo, after mention-
ing Socratic midwifery, says to Simplicio:

> If someone does not know the truth by himself, it is impossible
> for anyone to make him know it. I can indeed point out *things* to
> you, things being neither true nor false; but as for *the true—that is,
> the necessary; that which cannot possibly be otherwise*—every man
> of ordinary intelligence either knows this by himself or it is im-
> possible for him ever to know it. And I am sure that Salviati holds
> this opinion too. Therefore I tell you that the causes in the present
> problem are known to you, *but are perhaps not recognized as such*.[3]

This passage brings out very clearly the twofold idea that the
first principles of science are necessary rather than contingent,
and that knowledge of them is inborn rather than acquired, so
that it may be awakened but cannot be instilled. At another
place Salviati suggests to Sagredo and Simplicio that certain
propositions are 'already known' to them, 'though perhaps
without your realizing it'.[4]

---

[1] *TNS*, p. 4.   [2] p. 127.   [3] *TCWS*, pp. 157–8, my italics.
[4] *TCWS*, p. 12.

My last bit of evidence is a passage where Simplicio says to Salviati:

> I have frequently studied your method of arguing, which gives me the impression that you lean toward Plato's opinion that *nostrum scire sit quoddam reminisci* [our knowledge is a kind of recollection]. So please remove all question for me by telling me your idea of this.[1]

It would be nice if I could report that Salviati had replied: 'Indeed I do.' But at this point Galileo's epistemological caginess rather reasserted itself. Salviati replies that he will indicate what he feels about Plato's opinion by deeds rather than by words. He then proceeds, by means of a series of questions in the Socratic manner, to get Simplicio to 'remember' a fundamental physical truth. Instead of avowing Plato's idea of knowledge as reminiscence, he provides an exemplification of it.

Whether Hobbes read Galileo along these lines, I do not know. He may have done so; though it should be said that Hobbes's conception of *natural* philosophy is closer to Descartes' than to Galileo's: Hobbes saw the main task of the natural philosopher to be, not the discovery of principles (these being, for Hobbes, already sufficiently known), but the devising of hypothetical models showing how various natural phenomena may be produced (see below, pp. 69–70). But he did regard the principles and theorems of his *civil* philosophy in rather the same way that Galileo, if my account is right, regarded those of his natural philosophy.

§ 11   *Harvey*

Most of the ideas which went into Hobbes's method have now emerged; but two of them show up conspicuously only in

[1] *TCWS*, pp. 190–1; the editor, Stillman Drake, comments: 'This Socratic doctrine is a recurrent theme in Galileo's dialogues' (p. 478). A. Koyré, who stresses the Platonic character of Galileo's 'mathematicism', also quotes this passage and draws attention to Galileo's 'repeated mention . . . of the doctrine of reminiscence' ('Galileo and Plato', *Jour. Hist. of Ideas*, October 1943, p. 427).

Harvey's work. One of these has already made a brief appearance, after which we rather lost sight of it: the other has not yet appeared.

(1) Galileo's brilliant resolution of the trajectory of a projectile into constituent principles has tended to overshadow the older and less sophisticated idea of the resolution of a *thing* into physical parts or elements. The Paduan methodology was originally developed in the medical school in Padua[1] (which Harvey entered *circa* 1598); and there, 'resolution' originally meant physical dissection.[2] To an anatomist, taking a thing apart merely in thought sounds like armchair dissection.

The section on 'The Manner and Order of Acquiring Knowledge' in William Harvey's *On the Generation of Animals* opens in a Paduan vein: 'we proceed from things more known to things less known, from matters more manifest to matters more obscure';[3] and he goes on to quote the passage from Aristotle (see p. 52 above) which the Paduan school so often cited. We start, he says, with sensible wholes,[4] and in the case 'of our present subject' we proceed 'by repeated dissection'[5] to the discovery of principles. Harvey's notion of a biological principle differs importantly from Galileo's notion of a mechanical principle: a biological principle is an activating and controlling factor localized in some physical part of the organism. For instance, the chick 'arises and is constituted as it were by a principle or soul inherent in the egg';[6] again, in the case of snails, shrimps, etc., 'the beginning or principle of their life' is a 'pulsating vesicle' which in some cases can be *seen* as though 'through a window'.[7]

Hobbes's notion of political principles is nearer to Harvey's notion of biological principles than to Galileo's notion of mechanical principles: 'the principles of the politics consist in

---

[1] See Randall, *The School of Padua*, pp. 25 f.

[2] 'Resolution is twofold, natural or real, and logical. Real resolution . . . is strictly the separation and division of a thing into its component parts. Logical resolution is so called metaphorically' (Jacopo da Forti, quoted by Randall, p. 35).

[3] *Works*, p. 154.   [4] pp. 155–7.   [5] p. 158.   [6] p. 395.   [7] p. 30.

knowledge of the motions of the mind'.[1] These activating motions are, of course, localized in the individual parts of a civil society; and while outsiders cannot observe them, each individual can observe them in himself.

(2) With Galileo, composition was a logical (or mathematical) synthesis; with Harvey we get the idea (which goes back to Aristotle) that in piecing together a biological whole from a knowledge of its elements and principles one may recapitulate its history, indicate how it came to be what it is:

> ... in Animal Generation ... it appears advisable to me to look back from the perfect animal, and to inquire by what process it has arisen and grown to maturity, to retrace our steps, as it were, from the goal to the starting place; so that when at last we can retreat no further, we shall feel assured that we have attained to the principles; at the same time we shall perceive from what primary matter, and from what efficient principle, and in what way from these the plastic force proceeds.[2]

The compositive method turns into a genetic method.

Hobbes was concerned with the matter, generation and form of a strange artificial animal (a misbegotten monster, according to some), the 'great Leviathan'. He too retraces his steps from the goal to the starting place; but he was looking back from a diseased body politic;[3] and in *Leviathan* he recapitulates, not *its* history, but the rationalized history of a robust body politic.

---

[1] *De Corp* I, vi, 7 & *EW* i, p. 74.
[2] *Works*, p. 163.
[3] *Lev* pp. 167 f. & *EW* iii, pp. 308 f.

IV

Method and Politics

Hobbes's method determined the shape of his civil philosophy
—required it to start by stating what men's condition would be
were there no civil authority over them, and to go on to state
what rational measures they would have to take to escape
from that condition. And it thereby dictated Hobbes's democratic account of the origin of political authority. It also
determined the sort of prescriptive purpose his civil philosophy
should have, the kind of imperatives it should yield. These will
be the main conclusions of this chapter.

§ 12 *Artefacts and demonstrative science*

The claim that Hobbes was in the methodological tradition
outlined in the last chapter calls for some justification. After
remarking that one would expect Paduan methodology to
have had some influence in England, 'in view of the well-known
fact that many British medical and scientific men were trained
in the Italian universities in the sixteenth century', an Ameri-
can historian modestly suggests 'that Hobbes's views on
method, for example, may owe something to the thinking of
Italian Aristotelians'.[1] I shall now try to substantiate this
suggestion.

There is, Hobbes says,

> no method, by which we find out the causes of things, but is either
> *compositive* or *resolutive*, or *partly compositive*, and *partly*

[1] N. W. Gilbert, *Renaissance Concepts of Method*, 1960, p. 211.

resolutive. And the resolutive is commonly called *analytical* method, as the compositive is called *synthetical*.[1]

We use a method 'to proceed from known things to unknown ... But in knowledge by sense, the whole object is more known, than any part thereof'; so in the investigation of a given thing 'the beginning of our search is from the whole idea'. But to show why a thing is what it is we must begin with the causes of its parts:

> For the cause of the whole is compounded of the causes of the parts; but it is necessary that we know the things that are to be compounded, before we can know the whole compound. Now, by parts, I do not here mean parts of the thing itself, but parts of its nature.[2]

Hobbes adds that the 'common saying' that 'some things are more known to us, others more known to nature' does not 'mean that something is known to nature, which is known to no man'; by things 'more known to us, we are to understand things we take notice of by our senses'; by things 'more known to nature, those we acquire the knowledge of by reason; for in this sense it is, that the *whole*' is 'more known to us than the parts'.

Within this methodological tradition it was a disputed question whether, when writing a scientific treatise, one should confine oneself to a didactic, compositive (or 'synthetical') exposition, laying down first principles and proceeding deductively therefrom; or whether one should describe in a more personal and autobiographical way the resolutive (or 'analytical') procedures which led one to discover those principles. Galileo and Harvey inclined to the second way; and Descartes insisted that it is much superior. He granted that a synthetical exposition has a certain intellectual coerciveness which the other lacks: 'The reader, however hostile and obstinate, is compelled to render his assent'; but it does not satisfy 'the eager learner, because it does not show the way in which the

---

[1] *De Corp* I, vi, 1 & *EW* i, p. 66. [2] I, vi, 2 & p. 67.

matter taught was discovered'. An analytical exposition, by contrast, 'shows the true way by which a thing was methodically discovered', so that an attentive reader 'understands the matter no less perfectly and makes it as much his own as if he had discovered it himself'.[1]

Hobbes took a different view. It was Euclid's *demonstrative method*—his derivations of surprising theorems from undoubted axioms—which had fired him with the desire to emulate it in other fields. (Hobbes was quite disparaging about some of the *contents* of Euclid's *Elements*.)[2] The method of teaching, he says, is demonstration,[3] and 'the whole method . . . of demonstration is *synthetical*'.[4] In this respect, Hobbes is closer to Spinoza and Newton than to Harvey and Galileo. From the *Tract* to *Leviathan* his works open with a declaration of first principles and then magisterially unfold their implications.

That the methods of 'philosophy' (in Hobbes's sense; see p. 19 above) are resolution and composition implies, for Hobbes, that a philosophical account of something depicts a way in which it might have been *generated*: in recomposing it in thought one describes how it might have been generated in fact.

> The subject of Philosophy . . . is every body of which we can conceive any generation . . . or which is capable of composition and resolution . . .

And this entails that there can be no philosophical knowledge of anything ingenerable:

> Therefore it excludes *Theology*, I mean the doctrine of God, eternal, ingenerable, incomprehensible, and in whom there is nothing neither to divide nor compound, nor any generation to be conceived.[5]

[1] *PW* ii, pp. 48–9. I may perhaps add that I side with Descartes here.

[2] Euclid's definition of a straight line is, he said, 'inexcusable' (*EW* vii, p. 202); his definition of proportion is 'intolerable' (p. 207); and in his geometry 'there be some few great holes' (p. 245).

[3] *De Corp* I, vi, 10 & *EW* i, p. 79.

[4] I, vi, 12 & p. 81.   [5] I, i, 8 & p. 10.

God is indescribable.

Hobbes singles out three main kinds of generated things—geometrical figures, physical things and commonwealths—as the respective subjects of three main branches of philosophy: geometry, natural philosophy and civil philosophy. And he claims that in one important respect geometrical figures and commonwealths are like each other and unlike natural objects: a geometrical figure and a commonwealth are both, if in very different ways, human creations. And this similarity separates geometry and civil philosophy from natural philosophy: they are demonstrable whereas it is conjectural. Those branches of philosophy are demonstrable, he says, 'the construction of the subject whereof' is in our power; for here we do 'no more but deduce the consequences of' our 'own operation'.[1] If the causes are our own operations, we *know* the causes.

> The science of every subject is derived from a precognition of the causes, generation, and construction of the same; and consequently where the causes are known, there is place for demonstration, but not where the causes are to seek for. Geometry therefore is demonstrable, for the lines and figures from which we reason are drawn and described by ourselves; and civil philosophy is demonstrable, because we make the commonwealth ourselves. But because of natural bodies we know not the construction, but seek it from the effects, there lies no demonstration of what the causes be we seek for, but only of what they may be.[2]

True, we can be sure that any natural phenomenon has been produced by some sort of motion, 'for it is by motion only that any mutation is made in any thing'.[3] This, as we saw earlier (p. 43 above), is Hobbes's fundamental metaphysical principle. But we cannot know, in the case of a natural phenomenon, just what motion actually produced it:

> But seeing all effects are produced by motion, he that supposing some one or more motions, can derive from them the necessity of that effect whose cause is required, has done all that is to be expected from natural reason. And though he prove not that the

[1] *EW* vii, pp. 183–4.   [2] p. 184.   [3] p. 129.

thing was thus produced, yet he proves that thus it may be produced when the materials and the power of moving are in our
hands: which is as useful as if the causes themselves were known.[1]

In natural philosophy you can only propose a hypothetical
model from which, 'without contradictoin to any other manifest truth or experiment, you can derive' the effect you are
seeking to explain; and in examining your hypothesis 'you must
furnish yourself with as many experiments . . . as you can'.[2] At
the end of *De Corpore* Hobbes emphasizes that his accounts of
the generation of various natural phenomena are conjectural,
adding:

> Nevertheless, seeing I have assumed no hypothesis, which is not
> both possible and easy to be comprehended; and seeing also that
> I have reasoned aright from those assumptions, I have withal
> sufficiently demonstrated that they may be the true causes; which
> is the end of physical contemplation.[3]

As a preliminary summary of the differences Hobbes per-
ceived between natural philosophy on the one hand, and geometry and civil philosophy on the other, we may say, then,
that whereas the motions which produce natural phenomena
are external to us and generally hidden from us, the motions
which produce the geometrical figures we draw are the motions
of our own hands, and the motions which produce a commonwealth are the 'motions' of our own minds. Thus the generating
causes of the commonwealth may be known by any man 'that
will but examine his own mind'.[4]

This summary glosses over various complications and diffi-
culties. For one thing, if there is set before us a geometrical

---

[1] *EW* vii, pp. 3–4. See H. B. Acton, *The Illusion of the Epoch*, 1955,
pp. 55–6, for an account of the rather similar view of Engels that 'we prove
the correctness of our conception of a natural process by making it
ourselves'.

[2] *EW* vii, p. 88. The popular idea that Hobbes despised experiments
(jauntily affirmed by Pogson Smith in the Essay unhappily included in the
Oxford edition of *Leviathan*, p. viii) is incorrect. He only despised hap-
hazard experimenting; see also *EW* iv, pp. 436–7.

[3] *EW* i, p. 531.   [4] *De Corp* I, vi, 7 & *EW* i, p. 74.

figure—a circle, say—drawn in our absence, we can only conjecture about the way it was made:

> By knowing first what figure is set before us, we may come by
> ratiocination to some generation of the same, though perhaps not
> that by which it was made, yet that by which it might have been
> made.[1]

Nevertheless, our hypothetical account of the generation of the
circle before us is still superior to a hypothetical account of the
generation of, say, a thunderstorm. In the case of the circle we
can give a simple and, so to say, *typical* 'history' of it; and we
may claim that, however it was in fact drawn, it could not have
been drawn in a more economical and straightforward way
than the way we have given. But we could hardly make such a
claim for a hypothesis about a thunderstorm. This idea of a
typical or rationalized 'history' reappears in Hobbes's civil
philosophy.

A more serious difficulty is covered by Hobbes's over-terse
remark that 'civil philosophy is demonstrable *because we make
the commonwealth ourselves*'. The larger meaning of this will,
I hope, become clear later. Here I will only suggest that it
conflates two ideas. First, we 'make' the commonwealth in the
sense that it is composed or made up of the human beings
within it. Second, the sort of commonwealth we need can be
demonstrated by considering the commonwealth we would
make, in the stronger sense of 'institute' or 'construct', if we
were without one. We make this commonwealth in the double
sense that we are both 'the *matter* thereof, and the *artificer*'.[2]

§ 13 *Society decomposed and reconstructed*

Hobbes gave an informal account of his application of his
method to civil society in his Preface to the English translation
of *De Cive*:

> Concerning my method . . . I took my beginning from the very
> matter of civil government, and thence proceeded to its genera-

[1] *De Corp* I, i, 5 & *EW* i, p. 6.   [2] *Lev* p. 2 & *EW* iii, p. x.

tion and form, and the first beginning of justice. For everything is best understood by its constitutive causes. For as in a watch, or some such small engine, the matter, figure, and motion of the wheels cannot well be known, except it be taken insunder and viewed in parts; so to make a more curious search into the rights of states and duties of subjects, it is necessary, I say, not to take them insunder, but yet that they be so considered as if they were dissolved.[1]

To consider society as if dissolved is to imagine its members in a state of nature; and this is how Hobbes's civil philosophy opens. His account does not presuppose that such a state of nature has ever existed historically. It is an 'ideal' or limiting case in which every vestige of authority and organization has been imagined away, in which we

consider men as if but even now sprung out of the earth, and suddenly, like mushrooms, come to full maturity, without all kind of engagement to each other.[2]

Hobbes suggested that 'the savage people in many places of America' approximate to this condition.[3] But this does not matter for his argument; and he cheerfully conceded to Bishop Bramhall that 'it is very likely to be true, that since the creation there never was a time in which mankind was totally without society'.[4] Actually, Hobbes missed a pertinent historical example, here. According to Sextus Empiricus,

the shrewd Persians have a law that on the death of their king they must practise lawlessness for the next five days, . . . in order to learn by experience how great an evil lawlessness is, inflicting . . . murders and rapine and things which are, if possible, worse, so that they may become more trusty guardians of their kings.[5]

Hobbes's aim was the same, though he had to rely on only a vivid, hypothetical description of lawlessness to teach men to be trusty guardians of their commonwealth, so that it, unlike

[1] *EW* ii, p. xiv.   [2] *De Cive* viii, 1 & *EW* ii, p. 109.
[3] *Lev* p. 63 & *EW* iii, p. 114.   [4] *EW* v, p. 183.
[5] *Against the Professors* II, 33 & Loeb iv, pp. 205–7.

commonwealths hitherto, shall *not* be 'imperfect, and apt to relapse into disorder'.[1]

Taking a watch neatly to bits leaves its *parts* intact; only their arrangement is broken up. And taking a society to bits in thought leaves its members intact. Men in a state of nature are not primitive creatures. As Macpherson says, Hobbes's account of the state of nature depicts 'the behaviour to which men as they now are, men who live in civilized societies and have the desires of civilized men, would be led if all law and contract enforcement . . . were removed'.[2] Men in a state of nature possess language (see below, pp. 138–40) and religion, and they bandy moral epithets about. But these ideological factors only intensify their conflicts (see below, pp. 150–1). They are driven to devise a grand political remedy for all their conflicts, ideological as well as appetitive.

For reasons which we shall consider when we come to Hobbes's theory of human nature, men's 'natural' condition would be grim and frightening. It would force them to recognize their overwhelming need for a single all-powerful political authority. Part II of *Leviathan* tells the compositive story—gives a compressed and rationalized history of the way 'by which the parts of this body politic' are 'set together, and united'.[3]

It is implicit in Hobbes's resolutive-cum-compositive procedures that, however high and mighty the sovereign may be once established, his establishment is essentially democratic. To the 'question whether the magistrate's crown drops down on his head immediately from Heaven or be placed there by the hands of his subjects',[4] Hobbes's answer is predetermined by his method, reinforced by some of his other philosophical ideas. His resolutive method implies that in the imagined state of nature there is no civil order; and other of his philosophical

[1] *Lev* p. 176 & *EW* iii, p. 324.

[2] C. B. Macpherson, *The Political Theory of Possessive Individualism: Hobbes to Locke*, 1962, p. 22; and see H. Warrender, *The Political Philosophy of Hobbes*, 1957, p. 143.

[3] *Lev* p. 1 & *EW* iii, p. x.

[4] The phrase is from an unpublished treatise by Locke; see W. von Leyden (ed.), *John Locke: Essays on the Law of Nature*, 1954, p. 26.

ideas imply that there is no natural or moral order there, either.[1] Each man in a state of nature has nothing to go by but his own needs and calculations, no one to rely on but himself. He and the others create a sovereign out of a moral and political vacuum; his authority is entirely traceable to their needs and acts. 'We make a commonwealth', Hobbes says, by 'the act of our submission'; and there is 'no obligation on any man, which ariseth not from some act of his own'.[2] The sovereign's origins are humble and he never rises altogether above them. He is 'mortal, and subject to decay, as all other earthly creatures are',[3] and has in him 'many seeds of a natural mortality'.[4] Leviathan is something of a Frankenstein monster;[5] but he will perish if his makers turn against him (which they will do if he threatens their lives; see below, p. 137).

In Hobbes's time the idea of divine right was still widely held in one form or another. And he was widely accused of giving a *subversive* account of the sovereign as a merely man-made authority.[6] Clarendon, for instance, counter-advised the monarch 'for his greatness and security, never so far to lessen himself, as to be considered as the people's Representative';[7] and Richard Cumberland concluded his prolonged attack on Hobbes, *A Philosophical Enquiry into the Laws of Nature*, with the sentence:

> Whilst Mr. Hobbes with one hand speciously offers up to kings and monarchs royal gifts and privileges, he with the other, treacherously plunges a dagger into their very hearts.[8]

[1] We had a preliminary view of these latter implications towards the end of § 7. They will be more firmly established in § 22 and § 29.

[2] *Lev* p. 111 & *EW* iii, p. 203.   [3] p. 167 & p. 307.

[4] p. 114 & p. 208. As Warrender says, 'Leviathan is terrible' but he 'is also feeble' (*op. cit.*, p. 317).

[5] See R. G. Collingwood, *The New Leviathan*, 1947, pp. 88–9.

[6] See J. Dewey, 'The Motivation of Hobbes's Political Philosophy', in *Studies in the History of Ideas*, ed. Dept. of Philosophy of Columbia University, N.Y., 1918, vol. i.

[7] *Brief View . . . of . . . Leviathan*, 1676, p. 59. See below, p. 136, for a supporting argument which Clarendon drew from the sovereign's right to use the death-penalty.   [8] Dublin, 1751, p. 597.

Hobbes had claimed that his account of sovereignty 'repugns not the divine right'.[1] But I think that Clarendon and Cumberland were essentially right, here. Had Hobbes allowed that any human sovereign has his authority by divine right, he would presumably have allowed that Moses did; but this Hobbes expressly denied:

> It could not be the commandment of God that could oblige them [the Israelites]; because God spake not to them immediately, but by the mediation of Moses himself. . . . His authority therefore, as the authority of all other princes, must be grounded on the consent of the people.[2]

And near the end of *Leviathan* he claimed that its principles are 'true and proper' since he grounds the civil right of sovereigns 'upon the known natural inclinations of mankind'.[3] Hobbes, in effect, inverted the traditional Christian notion of political authority: not God above but the people below endow their sovereign with a quasi-divinity, make him a 'mortal god'. This anthropomorphosis of political authority was implicit in Hobbes's method.[4]

§ 14 *Reminding men of what they know*

It is usually when they have gone wrong that watches are taken to pieces. It was 'the disorders of the present time' which occasioned Hobbes's rational reconstruction of society (see p. 14 above). His aim was remedial and didactic: he wanted to teach rebellious men how to live peaceably together. The premisses from which he derived his didactic conclusions were

---

[1] *De Cive* Pref. & *EW* ii, p. xix. He also declared that the sovereign 'executeth his office of supreme pastor by immediate authority from God, . . . or *jure divino*' (*Lev* p. 296 & *EW* iii, p. 540).

[2] *Lev* p. 250 & *EW* iii, p. 464.

[3] p. 394 & p. 710.

[4] See the first quotation from Strauss on p. 32 above; and see Ernst Cassirer, *The Philosophy of the Enlightenment*, trans. Koelln and Pettegrove, Princeton, 1951, pp. 255–6.

psychological principles, i.e. *factual* premisses; and it has sometimes been alleged, for instance, by R. S. Peters,[1] that Hobbes
was guilty of the 'naturalistic fallacy' in trying to derive moral
conclusions from non-moral premisses. This accusation has
sometimes been countered unsatisfactorily. C. B. Macpherson
admits the derivation but denies its fallaciousness.[2] Yet the
objection to all such derivations is only an application of the
logical principle that a conclusion cannot be validly derived
from premisses if it has some content which is not contained
in them (as 'Socrates is a *snub-nosed* mortal' has some content
which is not contained in 'All men are mortal and Socrates is
a man'); and even the warmest admirer of Hobbes is ill-advised
to come to his rescue by throwing out this principle.

J. Plamenatz denies that Hobbes tried to *derive* his prescriptions from factual premisses.[3] But this clashes with Hobbes's
reiterated claim that *his* prescriptions, unlike those of previous
writers on moral philosophy and government, were not mere
exhortations or expressions of personal preference, but were
demonstrated by being deduced from principles which no one
can, upon reflection, honestly deny: namely, the known natural
inclinations of mankind.

My thesis is that Hobbes did derive his prescriptions from
factual premisses, but without committing a logical fallacy:
for his prescriptions are not *moral* prescriptions—they are more
like 'doctor's orders' of a peculiarly compelling kind. A
medical regimen may assume something of the appearance of
a stern moral code. It may require painful sacrifices. To live in

[1] R. S. Peters, *Hobbes*, 1956, pp. 170 f.

[2] 'His deduction of obligation from fact must be allowed a logical
validity' (*The Political Theory of Possessive Individualism*, p. 17; and see
pp. 81 f.).

[3] 'It has been objected against Hobbes that he tries to derive prescriptive statements from statements of fact. . . . The objection is wide of the
mark. . . . There is no inferring of rules of conduct from descriptive
statements' (Introduction to *Leviathan*, Fontana, 1962, pp. 12–13). But
Plamenatz appears to go back on this when he says later: 'What is perhaps
most impressive is the attempt made to explain how rules and obligations
arise from the desires and preferences of men' (p. 42).

accordance with it may require great determination. Lapses may be followed by remorse. But its sanction is not moral. It is prescribed in the patient's own interest.

The analogy between Hobbes's political prescriptions and doctor's orders is not exact. For one thing, medical science does not enable a doctor to *know* that his patient's overriding aim is to remain alive and healthy. For another, medical science does not enable the doctor to *demonstrate* to his patient the he must follow the prescribed regimen if he is to recover his health. The analogy becomes closer, however, if we suppose doctor and patient to be one person. An ill doctor whose overriding aim is to get well again, and who is convinced that he will do so only if he does x, will regard the prescription, 'Do x', as compelling.

That Hobbes's prescriptions should have an analogous character was implicit in his method, in conjunction with his idea of the knowability of his psychological principles. His resolutive-compositive method precluded any appeal to external norms, any importing of extraneous considerations into his civil philosophy. It confined him to the analysis of existing society into its indivisible parts; to the establishing of the principles which govern their behaviour; and to derivations from these. If this yields prescriptions or imperatives, these can only have been derived from those psychological principles.

The existing society which Hobbes took to pieces was a disordered society, torn by civil war. The society which he rationally reconstructed from a knowledge of the nature of its members was a well-ordered sovereign state. Now it has been objected that what comes out at the end of a resolutive-compositive enquiry should be the same as what went in at the beginning. I remarked on a previous occasion that when this method is applied to society the recomposed whole may very well differ from the original, that to apply the resolutive-compositive method to society is to discover what men *are* and what the state *ought to be* to be consistent with their nature.[1]
To this Macpherson has objected:

[1] *Philosophical Quarterly*, April 1955, p. 133.

> If men's natures . . . are such as to render them at war with each
> other, . . . men are consistent with their nature in so acting. . . .
> How can [Hobbes's composition of the elements] be called more
> consistent with their natures than the arrangement which actually
> exists . . .?[1]

An inverted version of this objection might also be made: if a
well-ordered sovereign state is alone consistent with human
nature, how is political disorder possible?

An analogy may help to dispel such objections. Suppose that
chess-player *A* finds himself being driven by *B* into increasingly
awkward positions until he is obliged to resign. *A* now recon-
structs the game to locate his first wrong move. He finds that it
was an early pawn move. He remembers why he made it; but
he also sees now why he should not have made it. His move
was consistent with his chess-playing personality at the time,
for then he was unaware of those unwanted consequences
revealed by the game and his reconstruction of it. But if he
were now to play *B* again, and the game were to open in just
the same way, it would be inconsistent for him to make the
same move again. What comes out of his rational reconstruction is not just the same as what went in: in explaining
how the old game went wrong it shows how it could have
gone better. It has prescriptive as well as explanatory implications for him.

Hobbes assumes that civil war is an unwanted condition.
The cause

> of civil war is, that men know not the causes neither of war nor
> peace, there being but few in the world that have learned those
> duties which unite and keep men in peace, that is to say, that have
> learned the rules of civil life sufficiently.[2]

Men on both sides at the outset of a murderous civil war find
themselves in a deteriorating situation inadvertently brought
about by themselves. They may have been behaving consistently, given their unawareness of the unwanted consequences

---

[1] *The Political Theory of Possessive Individualism*, p. 101.
[2] *De Corp* I, i, 7 & *EW* i, p. 8.

of their behaviour. But once aware of these, they would be mad to persist in such behaviour.

A further point may be brought out by a slight modification of our analogy. Suppose that *B* is teaching *A* chess, and that after their game *B* conducts a post-mortem, in which he shows that *A*'s initial mistake was that early pawn move. He has not exactly given *A* any factual information: when *A* made this move he either was fully informed of the positions of all the pieces or could have been so if he had examined the board more closely. Rather, *B* has drawn out implications of *A*'s (actual or potential) information at the time of that move, and this is something which *A* could, in principle, have done for himself at the time by the use of 'natural reason'. *B* has revealed to *A* something which *A* 'already knew' potentially. Clearly, it would be beside the point to retort that if *A* 'already knew' that this move was fatal he would not have made it; and it would be equally beside the point to object that, if men abhor civil war and can know by their natural reason how to avoid it, then civil war should never occur.

If we now suppose that *B* is *A*'s doctor and that *B* is telling *A* that his initial mistake was to eat those oysters, the situation is significantly different. We may assume that *A* did *not* 'already know' that the oysters would disagree with him when he ate them, that this was not an unnoticed implication of the information available to him at the time. In *this* respect the relation between Hobbes and his readers is more like that between chess-teacher and pupil than that between doctor and patient. He is not trying to instil any alien material—whether factual or moral—into their minds. They already possess all the needed material. He only draws attention to what they know already (or can know if they will but look into themselves) and draws out logical consequences of it. Near the beginning of the first version of his civil philosophy Hobbes announced that his intention was 'only to put men in mind of what they know already, or may know by their own experience'.[1]

Like Galileo, Hobbes leaned toward Plato's opinion that our

[1] *El of L* I, i, 2 & *EW* iv, pp. 1–2.

knowledge is a kind of recollection. He regarded Plato as the
best of the Greek philosophers,[1] and he said: 'To *know truth*,
is the same thing as to *remember*. . . . Neither was it rashly nor
unadvisedly said by Plato of old, *that knowledge was memory*.'[2]
Hobbes's view here was related to his theory of truth, a topic
we shall consider in § 28. Here I will only mention that for
Hobbes, as for Plato, rational knowledge of truths results from
a prior knowledge of *meanings*, and this prior knowledge
involves a kind of remembering. Hobbes's theory of meaning
is altogether different from Plato's, and so, consequently, is his
account of what happens when we 'remember' the meaning of
a word. But independently of this theory of meaning and truth,
the remembrance-theory fits Hobbes's *civil* philosophy very
well. His appraisal of its principles is analagous to Galileo's
appraisal of his. Hobbes regards them as empirically confirmed
by the correspondence between their consequences and
experience.[3] But we can also be jogged into *seeing* their truth.
These principles consist in a knowledge of the motions of our
minds. We may not have examined those motions honestly and
exactly; and when these psychological principles are first put
to us we may boggle at them. Hobbes himself admitted that
some people 'have a little been staggered' by them.[4] However,
if we obey the saying, 'Read thyself',[5] we shall come to find
them undeniable. And from these undeniable principles

[1] *Lev* p. 369 & *EW* iii, p. 668.

[2] *De Cive* xviii, 4 & *EW* ii, p. 304. For expository reasons I have dropped
some words of importance from this quotation. They are restored in
quotation (5) on p. 147 below.

[3] See the passage beginning: 'It may seem strange to some man, that
has not well weighed these things, that nature should thus dissociate, and
render men apt to invade, and destroy one another; and he may therefore,
not trusting to this inference made from the passions, desire perhaps to
have the same confirmed by experience. Let him therefore consider with
himself, when taking a journey, he arms himself . . .' (*Lev* p. 62 & *EW* iii,
pp. 113–14). However, as Clarendon pointed out (*Brief View . . .* p. 29),
this is really spurious confirmation, since the existence of only a *few*
highwaymen, etc., would prompt people to take the precautions Hobbes
describes.

[4] *De Cive* Pref. & *EW* ii, p. xxiii.   [5] *Lev*, p. 2 & *EW* iii, p. xi.

Hobbes's civil philosophy proceeds (or so he supposes) with the inexorability of a Euclidean demonstration to its didactic conclusions. It does not, except incidentally, provide new information or proffer advice or upbraid or exhort. It is an eye-opener; and once our eyes have been opened to our situation, we shall see that we *have* to swallow the bitter political medicine it prescribes.

V

Laws of Nature

Hobbes couched his imperatives in the traditional natural-law terminology. Thus our claim that his method determined the kind of imperatives his civil philosophy yielded implies that it determined the kind of laws of nature it invoked. In this chapter the thesis that his laws of nature do indeed have the character prescribed for them by his method will be upheld against an opposed thesis.

§ 15   *Assertoric hypothetical imperatives*

Laws of nature play a crucial role in Hobbes's civil philosophy. In an otherwise lawless state of nature it is they which require men to establish a sovereign authority over themselves. And although their importance diminishes once a system of civil law exists, they continue to play a by no means insignificant role; for it is they, rather than the sovereign's laws, which require him to make, and his subjects to obey, life-protecting laws.[1] A misappraisal of Hobbes's laws of nature would badly disorient one's interpretation of his civil philosophy.

Kant divided imperatives into categorical imperatives (which prescribe morally necessary actions) and hypothetical imperatives (which prescribe actions as practically necessary means to

---

[1] Howard Warrender, who emphasizes this continuing role of the laws of nature after the institution of civil society, adds to this that they also govern international relations, and citizens' conduct in areas not covered by civil law (*The Political Philosophy of Hobbes*, ch. vii).

some end); and he divided the latter into problematic hypothetical imperatives (which prescribe means to a possible end) and assertoric hypothetical imperatives (which prescribe means to an actual end).[1] The upshot of the previous chapter, then, is that Hobbes's laws of nature are assertoric hypothetical imperatives in Kant's sense; and since the fixed end for which they prescribe practically necessary means—namely, self-preservation or the avoidance of wounds and destruction—is an egocentric end dictated by a man's biological-cum-psychological make-up, this implies that Hobbes's laws of nature do not have a distinctively moral character.

Now Hobbes speaks of them as 'moral' laws. He says that they 'are called not only *natural*, but also *moral* laws',[2] that 'the true doctrine of the laws of nature, is the true moral philosophy',[3] and that transgression of these laws is iniquity.[4] But to take such remarks to mean that these laws have a moral as distinct from a prudential character would be like taking Copernicus's use of the term 'sunrise' to indicate that he had given up his heliocentric hypothesis. We have already noticed strong *reductionist* tendencies in Hobbes (p. 46 above). The aim of a philosophical reduction is to collapse a commonly accepted dichotomy (for instance, the mental/physical dichotomy) where the common view is that what lies on one side of the division is essentially different from what lies on the other. The popular dualism is usually reflected in two terminologies, each peculiar to one of the two domains. The reductionist's claim is that one of the two domains is really only a sub-domain of the other. His claim implies that it is in principle possible to dispense with the terminology peculiar to this sub-domain. But he may concede that in practice this would probably lead to fearful prolixity,[5] or even prove impossible to carry out. So the

---

[1] See *The Moral Law*, trans. H. J. Paton, pp. 82 f.

[2] *Lev* p. 148 & *EW* iii, p. 271.   [3] p. 80 & p. 146.   [4] *EW* vi, p. 26.

[5] In the *Principia Mathematica* of Russell and Whitehead, arithmetical notions are reduced to logical notions, but it would be well-nigh impossible to do any *sums* in the new logical terminology—in which, for example, '2' is replaced by '$\hat{\alpha} \left\{ (\exists x, y). x \neq y. \alpha = \iota\,{}^{\backprime}x \cup y \iota\,{}^{\backprime}y \right\}$'.

reductionist will prefer (in Agostino Nifo's famous phrase) to 'think with the learned, and speak with the vulgar'. That is, he will continue to use the theoretically otiose but practically indispensable terminology (just as Copernicus continued to speak of sunrise and sunset) though what he means by the statements he makes in this terminology will be rather different from what the 'vulgar' would have meant by them.

Hobbes's reductionist attitude to the moral-law/self-interest dichotomy is apparent in his very first statement (in the Epistle Dedicatory to *The Elements of Law*) about the laws of nature:

> To reduce this doctrine [of justice and policy] to the rules and infallibility of reason, there is no way, but first to put such principles down for a foundation, as passion not mistrusting, may not seek to displace; and afterward to build thereon the truth of cases in the law of nature (which hitherto have been built in the air) by degrees, till the whole be inexpugnable.[1]

In other words, the so-called 'moral' law, or law of nature, consists of precepts or general rules found out by rational derivation from principles to which all individuals, given their passionate make-up, will assent. This passage indicates clearly enough why Hobbes wanted to reduce morality to rational self-interest. It comes after a complaint to the effect that what had hitherto been written concerning justice and policy was full of 'controversies and dispute'; and he obviously felt that this would continue until the 'moral' law—the law that tells us how to live with other men—is securely anchored in our deepest wants. A merely moralistic 'law', not so anchored, would be *ineffectual* (a mere 'brooding omniscience in the sky' in Justice Holmes's phrase, 'built in the air' in Hobbes's phrase). According to Hobbes's psychology, if men did not need to obey the 'moral' law, they would not. If Hobbes's laws of nature were to be compelling they had to be derived from undeniable psychological principles; if his civil philosophy was to meet the problems posed for it by the civil wars, he had to

---

[1] *EW* iv, p. xiii.

collapse the ought/want dualism into a single system of basic
wants and proven hypothetical imperatives:

> A LAW OF NATURE (*Lex Naturalis*) is a precept or general rule,
> found out by reason, by which a man is forbidden to do that
> which is destructive of his life or taketh away the means of pre-
> serving the same; and to omit that by which he thinketh it may be
> best preserved.[1]

In recent years, however, a very different view of Hobbes's
laws of nature has gained currency. First sketched in a famous
article by A. E. Taylor in 1938,[2] it has since been modified and
systematized by Howard Warrender in a forceful and scholarly
work.[3] If the 'Taylor-Warrender thesis', as it is sometimes
called, were substantially right, my view, not just of Hobbes's
natural laws or even of his civil philosophy, but of his whole
system of ideas, would be badly wrong. This challenge must
now be taken up.

§ 16   *The Taylor-Warrender thesis*

Although Warrender's detailed picture of Hobbes differs importantly from Taylor's sketch, we may speak of a 'Taylor-
Warrender thesis', since some of Taylor's main ideas occupy
central positions in Warrender's book.[4] Taylor severed
Hobbes's 'ethical doctrine' concerning the laws of nature from
his egoistic psychology ('with which it has no logically necessary connection')[5] and hooked it to Hobbes's theism ('a certain
kind of theism is absolutely necessary to make the theory
work');[6] Taylor insisted that his laws of nature are not mere
'pieces of advice' about the prudent pursuit of self-interest;
they are *moral* laws which *dictate duties*,[7] and are obligatory
because they are *commanded by God*;[8] they constitute 'a very

---

[1] *Lev* p. 64 & *EW* iii, pp. 116–17.

[2] 'The Ethical Doctrine of Hobbes', *Philosophy*, October 1938 (to be
reprinted in *Hobbes Studies*, ed. K. C. Brown, 1965).

[3] *The Political Philosophy of Hobbes* (1957).

[4] Warrender, of course, makes due acknowledgements to Taylor.

[5] *Philosophy*, October 1938, p. 408.   [6] p. 420.   [7] p. 411.   [8] p. 418.

strict deontology',[1] whose theistic character places it beyond the ken of atheists.

Before pursuing these ideas into the ampler context which Warrender provides for them I will indicate how they clash with ideas in this book. First: Hobbes's account of political authority starts out from individual wants according to me, from God's commands according to Taylor. Second: I have emphasized that Hobbes wished to *demonstrate* the prescriptions embodied in his laws of nature, and that these were largely directed against the religious zealots of his day. Taylor's theistic interpretation of them can hardly be squared with this. Any Puritan opponent of Hobbes would have been confident that *he* understood God's commands better than did this disreputable theologian; moreover, he could have reinforced this by pointing to Hobbes's own assertion that there can be *no* knowledge of God beyond the bare fact that he exists (see above, p. 68). Taylor tried to circumvent this by suggesting that Hobbes could have used God's incomprehensibility to deprive his opponents of the right to deny that God commands what he, Hobbes, alleged that he commands.[2] But if Hobbes had objected to such an opponent: 'you are in no position to challenge my contentions about God's commands since you cannot know anything about God', his objection would obviously have boomeranged. Third: Taylor says that a public system of *moral* rules already exists in the state of nature, whereas I shall claim (in § 29 below) that Hobbes's theory of moral language implies that such a system can exist only when there is a sovereign. Fourth: my main thesis is that Hobbes's ideas hang together, whereas Taylor's thesis is that even Hobbes's civil philosophy is bifurcated into two contrasting and disconnected sub-systems, a theistic deontology and an egoistic psychology.

I will state the core of Warrender's thesis[3] in my own words

---

[1] *Philosophy*, 1938, p. 408.   [2] p. 422.

[3] Warrender sometimes provides alternative interpretations of Hobbes's position without deciding between them. I shall try to confine criticism to those interpretations to which he does commit himself.

in the form of a syllogism with whose major premiss (1) I agree and with whose minor premiss (2) and conclusion (3) I disagree.

(1) The laws of nature persist through the state of nature into civil society.[1]

(2) They are essentially *moral* laws[2] most of which prescribe *duties to society*[3] and are morally obligatory *because commanded by God*.[4]

(3) Therefore, moral laws are not created by the sovereign (his role is only to interpret, and render fully operative, pre-existing moral laws).[5]

If, as I claim, (3) is mistaken, (1) or (2) must be mistaken. Some commentators who reject (3) go on to reject (1), holding that Hobbes's so-called 'laws' of nature become *laws* only when enacted by the sovereign.[6] But our interpretation of them endorses (1). 'If you want to avoid violent death (and you do), you must live in submission to a sovereign arbitrator'— if such an assertoric hypothetical imperative is valid, it is valid whether or not one is living under a sovereign. I conclude that the guilty premiss is (2).

Warrender did not consider as an alternative to (2) the possibility that the laws of nature are more like doctor's orders. He assumed that any non-moralized interpretation of them would interpret them as merely describing 'how men do act' and not as prescribing 'how men ought to act'. On all non-moralized interpretations, according to Warrender, Hobbes is regarded

as having put forward a number of psychological principles . . . to the effect that men seek their own interest or self-preservation. . . . He may also point out that men are not always efficient or economical in pursuing these objectives, but he is able to offer no

[1] See *The Political Philosophy of Hobbes*, pp. 7, 11.
[2] p. 102 and *passim.*   [3] p. 218.   [4] pp. 98–9.   [5] pp. 28, 143.
[6] M. J. Oakeshott holds this. See his Introduction to *Leviathan* (Blackwell), pp. lix–lxi, and his *Rationalism in Politics*, 1962, pp. 268 and 273. The best evidence for this view is a passage in *Lev* p. 138 & *EW* iii, pp. 253–4, considered by Warrender on pp. 166 f. In § 18 I shall maintain that the laws of nature are laws because God is the author of nature.

further theory concerning whether they ought to pursue them or to be efficient in doing so.[1]

This is like claiming that medical science, being descriptive, does not permit prescriptions. But a theory which claims to describe the chief end which men do in fact pursue need not confine itself thereafter to describing their more or less inefficient pursuit of it: it may go on to prescribe the best way to attain that end.

In this chapter we shall be concerned with Warrender's minor premiss (2); his conclusion (3) will not be challenged until we consider Hobbes's theory of moral language in § 29. However, a comment is in place now on Warrender's interesting explanation for Hobbes's tendency 'to write as though the sovereign were himself responsible for the creation of obligations, where there were none before'.[2] Warrender introduces the term 'validating condition' to denote a condition which must be satisfied if a certain law is to be operative; if it is unsatisfied, the law is 'suspended'. For example: it is, for Hobbes, a law of nature 'that men perform their covenants made'; but this law is suspended if he who is to perform first 'has no assurance the other will perform after'.[3] Such assurance is a *validating condition* for this law. Now in the state of nature validating conditions usually *are* unsatisfied. Warrender suggests that this may give Hobbes's readers the impression that in it there are no moral laws, whereas Hobbes's real position is that there are, though most of them are in a state of suspended animation; and the sovereign's primary function, which is really to create validating conditions for the laws of nature, may likewise be mistaken for the creation of the moral laws themselves.

Now it makes only a verbal difference whether a law's validating conditions are listed separately, or incorporated into the law itself. Hobbes might equally have said that it is a *universally operative* law of nature 'that men perform their covenants made provided he that performeth first has assurance the other

<hr>

[1] p. 4.   [2] p. 144.   [3] *Lev* p. 68 & *EW* iii, p. 124.

will perform after'. *This* law would not be suspended where he who is to perform first lacks such assurance (a law that parked cars must have lights on at night in unlit streets is not *suspended* where there is all-night street-lighting).

When Hobbes came to his first, and 'fundamental', law of nature, he incorporated into it a clause, italicized in the following quotation, which might have been stated separately as a validating condition. He declared that

> it is a precept, or general rule of reason, that every man ought to endeavour peace *as far as he has hope of obtaining it; and when he cannot obtain it, that he may seek, and use, all helps and advantages of war.*[1]

This is not a severely *moral* law. It might have *sounded* more moral if Hobbes had detached the validating condition and stated it separately. But this would have been only a verbal change. One could, by exploiting Warrender's apparatus, transform a thieves' code into quite a moral-sounding system (its first principle might be 'Never steal'—together with the validating condition that there is a reasonable chance of being found out). A system of moral-sounding but suspendable laws is not a whit superior to the equivalent system of universally operative laws; with Warrender's admission that a validating condition for all Hobbes's laws of nature is that the agent has a sufficient motive to obey,[2] together with the fact that Hobbes's theory of motivation is essentially egocentric,[3] the colour rather drains out of Warrender's moralized picture of these laws.

§ 17 *Alleged dualism*

There are, Warrender claims,

> two systems in Hobbes's theory, a system of motives and a system of obligations. The system of motives ends with the supreme principle of self-preservation . . .; the system of obligations ends with the obligation to obey natural law regarded as the will of God.[4]

[1] *Lev* p. 64 & *EW* iii, p. 117. [2] pp. 23–5, 87 f., 97. [3] See § 21 below. [4] p. 213.

Moreover,

> there exists a considerable gulf between these laws [of nature] and
> the principles upon which Hobbes's natural man is motivated.[1]

I will begin with this alleged gulf; for if it is there, there must
indeed be two systems; and even if, as I shall argue, it is not,
there may still be two logically distinct but coinciding systems.
In § 18 I shall conclude that there is only one system.

Warrender bases a good deal on the fact that for Hobbes
'the fundamental law of nature is not "preserve thyself", but
"seek peace", and the further laws of nature are derived from
the latter precept'.[2] He feels that this gives them 'a more social
and less self-regarding appearance than is often associated
with Hobbes's theory'.[3] These peace-enjoining laws 'are not
maxims for personal success, nor even personal rules for
keeping alive'; they are 'concerned with the conservation of
society'; and they are, he quotes Hobbes as saying, 'contrary
to our natural passions'.[4]

That the fundamental law does not enjoin self-preservation
conforms at least as well with our interpretation of it as an
assertoric hypothetical imperative. Such an imperative does not
prescribe an *end*; it takes the end for granted and prescribes
practically necessary means to it. A doctor might say: 'First,
lay off alcohol. Second, take a long holiday. . . .' He would
hardly say: 'First, get well. Second, lay off alcohol. . . .'[5]

That Hobbes's first and fundamental law enjoins peace might
even be used *against* the theistic part of Warrender's interpretation. A natural lawyer like Puffendorf, who did give an essentially theistic account of the law of nature, says (as one would
expect) that the *first* part of that law 'gives us directions how . . .

----

[1] pp. 274–5.   [2] p. 216.   [3] p. 218.   [4] p. 275.

[5] Before Warrender, Taylor had likewise supported his moralized
interpretation with a contention which equally supports our interpretation. 'Hobbes', he said, 'agrees with Kant on the "imperative" character of
the moral law, exactly as he also agrees with him in the assertion that it is
the law of "right reason" ' (*Philosophy*, 1938, p. 409). But an assertoric
hypothetical imperative is also an imperative which may be found by
right reasoning.

man ought to behave himself towards *God*'.[1] But Hobbes's natural law, as Strauss points out, 'does not contain any prescription of duties towards God'.[2]

Hobbes did say that the laws of nature 'are contrary to our natural passions, that carry us to partiality, pride, revenge, and the like'.[3] I have no doubt that he meant by this that they are contrary, not to *all* our natural passions, but only to those that carry us to partiality, pride, revenge and the like; for there is one natural passion—namely, fear of wounds and unnatural death—which is ill-served by partiality, pride (see below, pp. 117–18) and hatred-inspiring revenge; and Hobbes says as clearly as one could wish that the law of nature is anchored in this passion.[4] It is true (and quite in accord with our interpretation) that it might be, as Warrender says, to one's 'immediate personal advantage to break this law'.[5] Hobbes himself says that 'most men, by reason of their perverse desire of present profit, are very unapt to observe these laws'.[6] But such non-observance is primarily *foolish* (rather than wicked or impious):

> The whole breach of the laws of nature consists in the false reasoning, or rather folly of those men who see not those duties they are necessarily to perform towards others *in order to their own conservation.*[7]

By Warrender's own admission, however deep the 'gulf' between Hobbes's psychology and morality may be, it has no width. Taylor had imputed to Hobbes an uneasy mixture—an egoistic psychology and a strict deontology which, however, *can require nothing out of line with the psychology*; and Warrender likewise admits that for Hobbes there can be 'no ultimate conflict between desire and duty',[8] and that 'the class of obligatory actions is always a sub-class of the actions that are

---

[1] *The Whole Duty of Man According to the Law of Nature* I, iii, 13.

[2] Leo Strauss, *What is Political Philosophy?* 1959, p. 184; and see *De Cive* xvii, 8 & *EW* ii, pp. 263–4.

[3] *Lev* p. 85 & *EW* iii, pp. 153–4.

[4] See, for example, the quotation on p. 85 above.

[5] p. 276.   [6] *De Cive* iii, 27 & *EW* ii, p. 45.

[7] ii, 1 n. & p. 16 n., my italics.   [8] p. 284.

in the interest of the individual'.[1] A critic of these two commentators has understandably protested: 'Warrender's and
Taylor's admission of Hobbes's feeling that no man can ever
act voluntarily without having as an object his own personal
good is the ruin of any attempt to put a truly moral construction on Hobbes's concept of obligation. . . . It deprives it of any
room to work'.[2]

But perhaps there are two nicely coinciding systems?
Following Taylor (see above, p. 85), Warrender supports this
with an appeal to Hobbes's distinction between *command* and
counsel: if his laws of nature were only 'maxims of prudence'[3]
they would have been mere counsel which the recipient may
decline to accept.[4]

Actually, at one point Hobbes does speak of

> all these precepts of nature derived by a certain artifice from the
> single dictate of reason *advising* us to look to the preservation and
> safeguard of ourselves.[5]

I agree, though, that they are not 'counsel' in Hobbes's sense;
and our interpretation does not imply that they are. One
receives counsel from someone else, and one may decline to
act on it. But Hobbes did not regard himself as offering
advice to his readers which they might, after due consideration, decline to follow; rather, he was reminding them of
what they already knew (see above, p. 79). For Kant, it is
true,

> imperatives of prudence, speaking strictly, do not command at
> all . . . they are rather to be taken as recommendations (*consilia*),
> than as commands (*praecepta*), of reason.[6]

---

[1] p. 220; and see pp. 208–9 and 272.

[2] Thomas Nagel, *Philosophical Review*, January 1959, p. 74.

[3] 'Maxims of *sapience*' would be the appropriate term; for as Warrender knows (*op.cit.*, pp. 242 and 269) prudence, for Hobbes, involves fallible
inductive beliefs formed by experience, whereas sapience involves rational
or scientific *knowledge* (*Lev* p. 22 & *EW* iii, p. 37).

[4] p. 204.

[5] *De Cive* iii, 26 & *EW* ii, p. 44, my italics.

[6] *Moral Law*, tr. Paton, p. 86.

But for Hobbes 'the language of desire and aversion is *imperative*; as *do this, forbear that*';[1] and he regarded aversion to violent death as men's overriding passion. A reader, jogged by Hobbes into seeing for himself that he must do x to avoid violent death, will regard 'Do x', not as a piece of advice well worth considering, but as an ungainsayable precept or imperative.

The idea of two independent but coinciding systems seems rather fishy. Why should Hobbes indulge in needless duplication? A man's reason dictates the way to his heart's desire; God dictates duties to him; why should these two sets of dictates, emanating from two such different sources, so nicely agree? Moreover, if Hobbes really does have two logically independent systems, he must, presumably, have a method of finding out the content of the second which is independent of his method of finding out that of the first (though leading to matching results). But what could this second method be? Since the second system consists of God's commands, the second method should, presumably, be a theological one. Now Warrender contends,[2] rightly as I believe, that it is not the scriptures which teach us what the laws of nature are (though they provide confirmation);[3] for one thing, the scriptures have to await the establishment, in accordance with natural law, of a sovereign before they receive an authoritative interpretation. And according to Hobbes, no rational theology is possible which could teach us what the laws of nature are. Warrender says early in his book that 'although our knowledge of God by reason is incomplete, it is sufficient to oblige us to obey his commands'.[4] Near the end of his book, however, he allows that 'rational knowledge of God is limited to the fact that he exists'[5] and that the content of the laws of nature 'is deduced neither from the attributes of God nor from the character of divine sanctions, for a substantial rational knowledge of these is impossible'.[6] To this we must add that reason, for Hobbes,

[1] *Lev* p. 29 & *EW* iii, p. 50. [2] pp. 226 f.
[3] See e.g. *De Cive* iv, 1–2 & *EW* ii, pp. 50–1.
[4] p. 82. [5] p. 308. [6] p. 309.

as well as being absolutely baffled by God's incomprehensibility, in any case has, by itself, no prescriptive capacity. Hobbes had insisted before Hume that the function of reason in practical life is to serve the passions, and that reason, by itself, cannot tell us what we ought to do: 'For the thoughts are to the desires, as scouts, and spies, to range abroad, and find the way to the things desired'.[1] Reason, when not guided by passion, is as ignorant of duties as it is of God; so we can have no rational knowledge of the laws of nature, *qua* moral laws willed by God, that is independent of our knowledge of them *qua* hypothetical imperatives. If anyone still insists that there are two systems, he should add that the divine-cum-moral one, far from being a logically independent and free-standing system, is only a pale reflection of the naturalistic system of hypothetical imperatives under the principle of self-preservation, and that the contents of the divine system are dictated by, and knowledge of its contents is parasitic on knowledge of, the contents of the naturalistic system.

§ 18   *God the author of nature*

Hobbes said on several occasions that what makes the laws of nature *laws* is their being commanded by God:

> These dictates of reason, men used to call by the name of laws, but improperly; for they are but conclusions or theorems concerning what conduceth to the conservation and defence of themselves; whereas law, properly, is the word of him that by right hath command over others. But yet if we consider the same theorems as delivered in the word of God, that by right commandeth all things; then are they properly called laws.[2]

His intention, here, seems plain. He wanted the laws of nature to be compelling for everybody. Now for most people, a prescription will be compelling if observance of it is demonstrably

[1] *Lev* p. 35 & *EW* iii, p. 61.
[2] *Lev* p. 80 & *EW* iii, p. 147; and see *De Cive* iii, 33 & *EW* ii, pp. 49–50 and *El of L* I, xvii, 12 & *EW* iv, p. 109.

necessary for physical survival. But in Hobbes's time religious extremists were preaching that God required Englishmen to overthrow their king; and Hobbes agreed that it would be only rational to disobey one's civil sovereign *if* one would otherwise be punished eternally by God.[1] Thus if the prescriptions of his civil philosophy were to be compelling for all sorts of theists as well as for agnostics and atheists, he had to eliminate the very possibility of conflict between the dictates of reason and the commands of God. And this he could do very easily—almost by a stroke of the pen. For 'these dictates . . . proceed from nature'; and nature is 'the art whereby God hath made and governs the world'.[2] The dictates of reason prescribe necessary means to the end of self-conservation. This end is dictated by our human nature (see below, p. 117). Therefore it is willed by the author of nature; and he who wills the end, wills the means that are necessary to it. Therefore God wills these dictates of reason: they are not only *natural* but *laws*[3]— assertoric hypothetical imperatives stamped with divine authorship.

This suggests that Warrender mistook the theological top layer of a single system for a separate system existing alongside what is really its psychological or naturalistic basis; and it explains why his 'two systems' automatically coincide despite the 'considerable gulf' between them, and why there is no separate method for discovering the content of the divine-cum-moral system—whatever is required by nature is *ipso facto* commanded by God.

[1] 'The most frequent pretext of sedition . . . in Christian commonwealths, hath . . . proceeded from a difficulty . . . of obeying at once both God and man. . . . When a man receiveth two contrary commands, and knows that one of them is God's, he ought to obey that. . . . If the command [of his civil sovereign] be such as cannot be obeyed, without being damned to eternal death; then it were madness to obey it' (*Lev* p. 321 & *EW* iii, pp. 584–5).

It may be mentioned that for Hobbes *life eternal* meant everlasting bodily life on earth after the day of resurrection, while *torment eternal* meant simply 'everlasting death'. See *Lev* ch. 38.

[2] *Lev* p. 1 & *EW* iii, p. ix.

[3] pp. 185–6 & p. 343.

It seems to me that in laboriously taking apart what Hobbes
had welded together, Warrender goes against Hobbes's whole
intention. Hobbes was invariably opposed to anything which
tended to make men '*see double*, and mistake their lawful
sovereign'.[1] If Hobbes had conceded that there are two systems
which logically could diverge though they happen not to, he
would have made it that much easier for religious zealots to
affirm that they actually do diverge (see above, p. 16). His whole
tendency was monistic: he sought to reduce all varieties of
prescription to one unequivocal system, so that rational self-
interest, moral obligation, divine command and the Bible
(authoritatively interpreted) necessarily pointed in the same
direction; and this single system comprised the laws of nature:

> They are called the laws of nature, for that they are the dictates
> of natural reason; and also moral laws, because they concern
> men's manners and conversation one towards another; so are
> they also divine laws in respect of the author thereof, God
> Almighty; and ought therefore to agree, or at least, not to be
> repugnant to the word of God revealed in Holy Scripture.[2]

The Taylor-Warrender thesis has startling implications for
Hobbes's view of the position of the atheist in civil society. On
our interpretation, the atheist's position will not differ importantly from the believer's: a clear-headed atheist, although he
will not regard the so-called 'laws of nature' as divinely
solemnized, will nevertheless regard them as *dictates* of reason
which minister to his profound desire to stay alive. (On this
interpretation, the target of Hobbes's statement that the dictates of natural reason are, moreover, willed by God was
people suffering from too much, rather than too little,
religious enthusiasm.) According to Warrender, on the other
hand, the atheist's position is one of total alienation:

> The atheist is not simply a criminal or a sinner; he exists outside
> the competence of natural law completely, in a state of nature or
> war much more fundamental than the Hobbesian State of Nature
> obtaining before the institution of civil society.[3]

[1] *Lev* p. 248 & *EW* iii, p. 460.   [2] *El of L* I, xviii, 1 & *EW* iv, p. 111.
[3] p. 316.

Warrender shows that this is indeed an implication of the theologized position he ascribes to Hobbes; and he claims, on the basis of a passage in *De Cive*, that Hobbes explicitly endorsed this implication. In this passage Hobbes says that the atheist is a fool and an enemy of God and may 'be justly punished both by God, and supreme magistrates'.[1]

In considering this we should remember that Hobbes knew that he was widely suspected (however unjustly) of atheism himself. Part of his intention, at least, in writing this was surely to repel such suspicions. Was it also his intention to encourage supreme magistrates actually to punish atheists? Fortunately, this can be answered without raising the vexed question of the sincerity of Hobbes's theism.[2] As we shall see in the next section, it was an important part of Hobbes's theory of mind that one man can never know what another man's inner beliefs really are; and anyone forcibly required to confess what his beliefs are has a right to say whatever is most likely to clear him.[3] Thus the right which Hobbes, in *De Cive*, gives the sovereign to punish atheists is an empty right: a charge of atheism could never be proved. And in *Leviathan* even this empty right is no longer given. There, after emphasizing that the sovereign 'hath supreme power in all causes, as well ecclesiastical as civil . . .' he adds: '. . . as far as concerneth actions and words, for those only are known and may be accused'.[4] In connection with this alleged outlawing of atheists,

[1] xiv, 19 n. & *EW* ii, pp. 198–9 n.

[2] S. I. Mintz has made a good point against Strauss and others who claim that it was insincere: 'It is hard to credit such a theory [that Hobbes's 'theism' was a screen thrown up for his own safety] when we remember that Hobbes's *openly-avowed* opinions on the nature of God were profoundly unorthodox and aroused the most intense opposition. . . . If safety and a peaceful life were his object he would have had to express his opinions far more circumspectly' (*The Hunting of Leviathan*, 1962, p. 44). See also K. C. Brown, 'Hobbes's Grounds for Belief in a Deity' (*Philosophy*, October 1962). Since Brown rather suggests (p. 336) that opponents of Warrender's views have to impugn the sincerity of Hobbes's theism, I may mention that its insincerity is *not* presupposed by my criticism of the Taylor-Warrender thesis.

[3] *Lev* p. 70 & *EW* iii, p. 128. [4] p. 300 & p. 547.

D

Warrender departs from his claim that there is sufficient support in *Leviathan* alone for the views in his book.[1] One is tempted to make to him the retort which Hobbes made to Bishop Bramhall about a criticism (in the latter's *Catching of the Leviathan*) of that very passage in *De Cive*:

> He saw he could not catch *Leviathan* in this place, he looks . . . in my book *De Cive* . . . to try what he could fish out of that.[2]

It is not only because I should have had to scrap the thesis of this book that I should have been disappointed if Warrender's thesis had withstood criticism. My feeling was expressed by a remark made by Peter Munz:[3] 'Warrender is most impressive. But . . . the older picture of Hobbes is so much more *interesting*. If Warrender's picture of Hobbes is right, I would almost feel that it is time we stopped being so interested in Hobbes and started being interested in whoever invented the older picture of Hobbes.' The essence of the older picture was perhaps caught by Hegel when he said that Hobbes, unlike his predecessors who appealed to extra-human principles, 'sought to derive the bond which holds the state together, that which gives the state its power, from the principles which lie within us, which we recognize as our own'.[4] According to the older picture, Hobbes showed how men, although nature dissociates them and renders them apt to invade and destroy one another,[5] are nevertheless able, without supernatural assistance, each proceeding under his own steam and using his own natural faculties, to build a peaceful society for themselves.

In contrast to this anthropocentric political philosophy— this 'do-it-yourselves' theory of the state—the traditional natural-law theorists regularly called in God to lay down natural laws and punish hereafter those transgressors who do not get their deserts on earth. As Warrender, who regards 'the

---

[1] p. vii.   [2] *EW* iv, p. 295.

[3] In a letter to the author, 7 June 1961.

[4] *Hegel's Lectures on the History of Philosophy*, tr. E. S. Haldane and F. H. Simpson, 1896, iii, p. 316.

[5] *Lev* p. 62 & *EW* iii, pp. 113–14.

sanction of salvation' as essential to Hobbes's system,[1] all too truly remarks,[2] 'the traditional natural-law theorists would not have quarrelled overmuch' with the Hobbesian laws of nature (as interpreted by Warrender). He has turned Hobbes into the systematizer of an elderly tradition, into a thinker to be set beside Hooker as a major precursor of Locke, the essence of his political theory being that the state of nature is pervaded by a moral law, handed down by God, which requires only interpretation and enforcement by the civil authority, and that atheists are beyond the pale. Locke would have been amazed at this assimilation.[3]

---

[1] p. 277.   [2] p. 311.

[3] Perhaps this is really only a case of *plus ça change*. . . . For in the meanwhile, Locke scholars have been refashioning their man; and the new Locke bears a peculiar resemblance to the old Hobbes. According to Richard Cox, Locke's 'conception of the state of nature—whether with regard to individuals or states—is in fact fundamentally Hobbesian in character'; and Locke, though he seems to follow Hooker, was 'in fact subscribing to and promoting the radically modern version of natural law which is developed in the writings of Hobbes' (*Locke on War and Peace*, 1960, pp. xix–xx). This situation is painful for examination candidates liable to be asked to 'compare and contrast' Hobbes and Locke. So let us all agree to the following compromise: Hobbes was a moralizing natural lawyer in the Hooker tradition, while Locke preached a mixture of egoism, fear, and authority; and Hobbes wrote *The Second Treatise*, while Locke wrote *Leviathan*.

VI

Human Nature

Hobbes's theory of human nature consists of psychological truisms—men laugh, feel pity, are averse to being killed, etc.—vigorously reinterpreted in the light of certain psychological principles. These principles of his, which put the spice into his theory, are predominantly metaphysical, and grow out of his materialist metaphysics combined with some of the biological ideas of William Harvey. These psychological principles enabled him to go beyond his knowledge of himself and his observations of others to a general theory of man sufficiently powerful to do what was required of it within his civil philosophy. All that will be the thesis of this chapter.

§ 19   *Problems and desiderata*

One thing his theory of human nature had to do was to establish the possibility of knowledge of the inner workings of other men's minds. Hobbes had to depict how men *would* behave in a state of nature; he could hardly infer this from observations of men's more or less restrained behaviour in organized society; he needed a psychological *theory* which he could combine with the counter-factual supposition that there is no social organization. And the sovereign needs this same inside knowledge of men:

> He that is to govern a whole nation, must read in himself, not this or that particular man; but mankind.[1]

[1] *Lev* p. 2 & *EW* iii, p. xii.

If the sovereign knew nothing of the inside workings of his subjects' minds, his legislative control over them would be groping and uncertain. He would be like a policeman in charge of a madhouse, always afraid that his inscrutable subjects would unaccountably turn on him.

Now the possibility of such inside psychological knowledge seems distinctly problematic within Hobbes's system. For Hobbes regarded thinking as an activity which goes on inside one's head,[1] and which is therefore unobservable to outsiders. And since the connection between inner thinking and outward behaviour is, for Hobbes, contingent and variable, it is impossible for you to read my thoughts by watching my outward behaviour. Each of us is condemned to solitary confinement within his body.[2] We can transmit and receive signals through the walls of our cells, and we may even work out and execute a common plan. But our minds never meet. Hobbes's position here is the exact contrary of that of his critic Cudworth, who wrote:

> A man cannot apprehend himself as a being standing by itself, cut off, separated, and disjointed from all other beings, . . . but looks upon himself as a member lovingly united to the whole system of all intellectual beings.[3]

Hobbes's privacy-thesis, as we may call it, has important implications for his civil philosophy. It obviously contributes to the desolate picture he draws of men's isolation and self-dependence in a state of nature. For most of us, few punishments could be more terrible than to be deprived of all human company. But for Hobbes, a person does not really meet other people anyway, but only experiences the effects they produce within his body; if those effects are mainly unpleasant, as they would be in a state of nature, he would rather be by himself.

[1] Thoughts 'are nothing really, but motion in some internal substance of the head' (*El of L* I, vii, 1 & *EW* iv, p. 31).

[2] See M. J. Oakeshott's Introduction to *Leviathan* (Blackwell), p. liv.

[3] Quoted by J. A. Passmore in his *Ralph Cudworth*, 1951, p. 72.

Men have no pleasure, but on the contrary, a great deal of grief, in keeping company, where there is no power able to over-awe them all.[1]

Hobbes's privacy-thesis also has a happier implication (touched on above, p. 97): it rules out Nocturnal Councils and Grand Inquisitors. Only God 'knoweth the heart', and human governors can take no notice of 'the inward thought and belief of men'.[2] If an inquisitor doubts the sincerity of a man's outward expressions, further probing and questioning will not discover the beliefs themselves; it will only provoke further outward expressions. The inquisitor's quarry forever eludes him. Thus it is futile to try

> to extend the power of the law, which is the rule of actions only, to the very thoughts and consciences of men, by examination, and *inquisition* of what they hold.[3]

What concerns us now, however, is the desideratum thus created for Hobbes's theory of human nature, namely to show how, despite the privacy-thesis, the knowledge of other minds required by his civil philosophy is attainable.

Further desiderata were created by the picture he needed to give of the state of nature. Obviously, his civil philosophy could never get started if life in the state of nature were either charmingly pastoral or else so terrible that it drove any survivors to hopeless despair. It should be about as bad as it could be without depriving the survivors of the will and ability to get themselves out of it. This means that, however strong may be men's conflict-engendering passions, there must be a stronger passion which inclines them to put a stop to it all. Given such a conflict-stopping passion, Hobbes could safely depict the rest of their nature in a conflict-maximizing, or near-maximizing, way. I am saying, not that Hobbes arrived at his theory of human nature by calculating backwards in this

---

[1] *Lev* p. 61 & *EW* iii, p. 112.

[2] p. 249 & p. 462.

[3] p. 378 & p. 684; and see p. 285 & p. 518, and *El of L* II, vi, 3 & *EW* iv, p. 172.

way (we are concerned with his ideas rather than how he thought of them), but that it does in fact meet this desideratum.

Conflict-maximization requires men to be unlike in some respects, alike in others. With regard to political and religious idealizing, *diversity* fosters conflict.[1] With regard to desires for scarce resources, *uniformity* fosters conflict.[2] And, of course, the more conflict there is, the scarcer resources are.[3]

In § 29 we shall find that Hobbes's ethical subjectivism has precisely the effect of making appetitive uniformity engender ideological diversity. Now, we shall investigate his idea that men are psychologically uniform. He could not claim to have established this inductively; for according to the privacy-thesis he could not tell, from other people's behaviour, whether their minds worked like his or not. His uniformity-principle, if it was not to be a merely dogmatic postulate, required support of a more theoretical character. It got this from the twofold idea that *the mind is body-dependent and the body is heart-centred.*

In the next three sections it will be argued that Hobbes's theory of human nature, which incorporates this twofold idea, is largely metaphysical (in the sense indicated above, pp. 21–2), though stiffened by some of Harvey's scientific ideas; that this theory yields a uniformity-principle and also what may be called an egocentricity-principle, both principles having a metaphysical character; that the theory, in virtue of that scientific stiffening, also has predictive implications; and that

[1] 'There are no wars so sharply waged as between sects of the same religion, and factions of the same commonweal, where the contestation is either concerning doctrines or politic prudence' (*De Cive* i, 5 & *EW* ii, pp. 7–8).

[2] 'But the most frequent reason why men desire to hurt each other, ariseth hence, that many men at the same time have an appetite to the same thing; which yet very often they can neither enjoy in common, nor yet divide it' (i, 6 & p. 8).

[3] 'In such a condition [of war], there is no place for industry; because the fruit thereof is uncertain: and consequently no culture of the earth; no navigation, nor use of the commodities that may be imported by sea; no commodious building; no instruments of moving, and removing, such things as require much force. . . .' (*Lev* p. 62 & *EW* iii, p. 113).

this whole theory satisfies the desiderata mentioned above, concerning the knowability of other minds and the conflict-ridden condition of men in a state of nature.

§ 20   *Uniformity*

Hobbes took it for granted that all human bodies have a similar structure, are engines of the same type:

> For what is the *heart*, but a *spring*; and the *nerves*, but so many *strings*; and the *joints*, but so many *wheels*, giving motion to the whole body, such as was intended by the artificer?[1]

For a dualist like Plato, biological uniformity by no means implies a corresponding psychological uniformity: roughly similar bodies might be controlled by souls of essentially different grades. But Hobbes was a materialist who claimed that psychological phenomena *are* bodily activities. Anyone who finds this an impossible identification had better substitute for Hobbes's materialism the dualist doctrine which comes closest to it, namely epiphenomenalism, according to which psychological phenomena are insubstantial shadows cast by bodily goings-on. Both materialism and epiphenomenalism exclude Plato's idea that bodily movement can be initiated by a non-physical soul. They also exclude Descartes' idea that bodily movements can be redirected by the soul. Both imply that if two people—identical twins, say—were ever in exactly the same bodily state, then they would be in the same psychological state too. More generally, both imply, given that men's bodies work in the same way, that their 'minds' also work in the same way.

Between engines of similar structure there may be considerable variations in power, speed and performance. Hobbes allows that there can be a considerable 'difference of quickness' in the working of different men's minds.[2] And there may also be

[1] *Lev* p. 1 & *EW* iii, p. ix.

[2] Natural wit involves 'celerity of imagining' as opposed to what 'is commonly called dulness, stupidity, and sometimes by other names that signify slowness of motion, or difficulty to be moved' (p. 32 & p. 56).

considerable differences between what men want, as we shall see in a moment.

Hobbes laid down what we may call a *uniformity-principle* at the beginning of *Leviathan*.

> Whosoever looketh into himself, and considereth what he doth, when he does think, opine, reason, hope, fear, &c., and upon what grounds; he shall thereby read and know, what are the thoughts and passions of all other men upon the like occasions. . . .

This appears to imply that if I love chocolates, then everybody does. But this appearance is removed in the next sentence:

> . . . I say the similitude of *passions*, which are the same in all men, desire, fear, hope, &c.; not the similitude of the *objects* of the passions, which are things desired, feared, hoped, &c.[1]

Clarendon objected that with these 'subsequent words' Hobbes 'reduces that general proposition to signify . . . very little'.[2] We might re-state Clarendon's objection by saying that with these subsequent words Hobbes reduces a false empirical proposition to an unfalsifiable metaphysical proposition. For suppose that *A* displays a passion—greed, say—which seems to be entirely lacking in *B*: Hobbes's uniformity-principle, as so far stated, would then imply that *B*, despite appearances, is really greedy too, though apparently he has not so far encountered any of the objects which would excite his greed.

It is worth pursuing this idea into the writings of David Hume, for a moment; for he propounded a uniformity-principle essentially similar to Hobbes's; and as his cheerfully dogmatic statement of it proceeds, its metaphysical status becomes increasingly apparent.

If someone were to advance the claim that 'no single thing is so like another, so exactly its counterpart, as all of us are to one another'[3] as an *empirical* hypothesis, the most promising way of testing it might be to study people far away in time or

---

[1] p. 2 & *EW* iii, p. xi.
[2] *Brief View* . . . p. 11.
[3] The wording is Cicero's (*De Legibus* I, x, 29 & Loeb, p. 329).

place. But Hume assures you that you can find out about far-away people just as well by staying at home and studying the people there:

> Would you know the sentiments, inclinations, and course of life of the Greeks and Romans? Study well the temper and actions of the French and English. . . . Mankind are so much the same, in all times and places, that history informs us of nothing new or strange in this particular. Its chief use is only to discover the constant and universal principles of human nature. . . .

But suppose an historian or an explorer *were* to inform us of something 'new or strange'—would not this disturb the uniformity-principle? Not at all:

> We should immediately, from these circumstances, detect the falsehood, and prove him a liar, with the same certainty as if he had stuffed his narrations with stories of centaurs and dragons, miracles and prodigies. And if we would explode any forgery in history, we cannot make use of a more convincing argument, than to prove . . . that no human motives, in such circumstances, could ever induce him to such conduct.[1]

The principle is not to be tested against reports of strange goings-on in faraway places; *they* are to be tested against it. It enjoys a privileged, regulative status.

But suppose you went exploring and yourself observed actions which seemed undeniably 'irregular and extraordinary'; no doubt, if you reported what you had observed, readers back at home would dismiss your report as a traveller's tale; but would you not have disconfirmed the uniformity-principle to your own satisfaction, at least? Not according to Hume; for while these actions may 'seem to have no regular connexion with any known motives',[2] you may be confident that they have actually been produced by ordinary motives whose operation has been distorted by peculiar situational factors of which you are unaware: 'the most irregular and unexpected resolutions of men may frequently be accounted for by those who know every particular circumstance'.[3]

[1] *Enquiries*, pp. 83–4.   [2] p. 86.   [3] p. 88.

Lastly, suppose that you detect some 'irregular and un-expected' motive in *yourself*—would not *that* necessarily refute the principle for you? Hume could have resisted such a rebuttal in either of two ways. He might have claimed that your having this motive means that others have it too; but, perhaps because they are ashamed of it, they hide it from each other, so that each thinks he is peculiar in having it. Or he might have treated your admittedly eccentric motive in the same sort of way as he treated eccentric actions, namely as the joint product of a normal motive combined with, in Hume's phrase, 'the secret operation of contrary causes'[1]—a normal motive plus peculiar situational beliefs of which you may be unconscious. (By obstinately continuing to apply Hume's uniformity-principle to increasingly recalcitrant situations one event-ually gets, not altogether surprisingly, somewhere near the rudiments of the one modern psychological theory which denies that there are different psychological types, namely Freud's.)

By itself, Hobbes's uniformity-principle is no stronger than Hume's; it does not enable anyone to make genuine predictions about other people's thoughts and passions on the basis of his own. Still, the idea that men are essentially alike does provide the necessary framework for his theory of human nature which goes on to say *what* they are like—for one thing, they are all essentially egocentric.

§ 21 *Egocentricity*

Harvey's account of the human body is, broadly speaking, mechanistic, except for one central item: the heart itself is pictured as a life-giving pump which is self-moving and has no engine to drive it: it is 'the prime mover in the body of man'.[2] Rather as Kepler had regarded the sun as 'the first mover' in the solar system, controlling his satellites without being under mechanical control himself, so Harvey declared that the heart

[1] *Enquiries*, p. 87.   [2] *Works*, p. 4.

is the beginning of life; the sun of the microcosm, even as the sun in his turn might well be designated the heart of the world; . . . the heart . . . is the household divinity which . . . nourishes, cherishes, quickens the whole body, and is indeed the foundation of life, the source of all action.[1]

But in these passages Harvey was speaking only of men's bodily constitution; and he allows that the heart is to some extent influenced by something which he perhaps regarded as, in a way, superior to it, namely mind. Had he regarded the heart as sovereign over the mind too, he would have said that a feeling of fear, say, is the effect (or epiphenomenon or reflection or shadow) of a causally (though not necessarily temporally) prior physical agitation of the heart; that it is, say, because one's heart pounds that one consequently feels afraid. In fact he said that the mental change is causally and even temporally prior, and 'is the cause of an agitation whose influence extends to the heart, and there induces change . . .'[2]

Hobbes out-Harveyed Harvey in the supremacy he gave to the heart. He regarded the heart as the controlling organ, not just in the body, but in the whole man: his heart determines what a man perceives, what he feels, and what he desires.

Hobbes regarded the heart as 'the fountain of all sense'.[3] Why should he suppose that the heart is involved in, say, visual perceiving? Hobbes's reason seems to have been this. The pressure exerted through the medium by an external object on the perceiver's eye at first causes the fluids in the optical nerves to tend *inwards*; the resulting phantasm, however, seems to the perceiver to be 'situate without';[4] and this seeming outwardness, Hobbes apparently supposed, can be accounted for only

---

[1] *Works*, p. 47. Elsewhere, Harvey says that 'the heart, like the prince in a kingdom, in whose hands lie the chief and highest authority, rules over all; it is the original and foundation from which all power is derived, on which all power depends in the animal body' (p. 83).

[2] p. 70.

[3] *De Corp* IV, xxv, 4 & *EW* i, p. 392.

[4] IV, xxv, 2 & p. 391.

on the assumption that the fluids in the optical nerves are tending *outwards*; their tendency must be *reversed* before it can generate a phantasm of the object; and it will be reversed only when the externally stimulated pressure reaches the heart; the phantasm is caused, not directly by the stimulus of the distant body, but by the reaction of the heart to this stimulus.

Normally, a man's eyes, ears and other sense-organs are subjected to a great variety of pressures; and, according to Hobbes, phantasms are generated, not by every tiny reaction to each of these, but by the heart's *predominant* reactions. This qualification enabled Hobbes to account for perceptual selectivity; and also for memories and dreams. A phantasm-engendering disturbance does not die away upon the removal of the external stimulus, though it will probably be damped down and smothered by new disturbances caused by new stimuli. But subsequently, during a lull, this subdued disturbance may once more become predominant, and so engender a pale phantasm or memory-image.[1] Something similar happens in dreams, except that here old images get confounded and succeed one another incoherently.[2] It can also happen that in sleep 'some distemper of some of the inward parts of the body' sets up a disturbance in the nervous system approximating that which would have been caused in a waking observer by some external object; in which case he will dream that he sees (or hears) such an object.

This theory was useful to Hobbes for debunking claims to divine inspiration made by seditious preachers.[3] A religious

[1] 'In memory, the phantasms . . . are as if . . . worn out with time' (*De Corp* IV, xxv, 8 & *EW* i, p. 398).

[2] IV, xxv, 9 & pp. 399–402.

[3] See *Lev* pp. 156, 196 and 205 & *EW* iii, pp. 286–7, 361 and 379. An amusing instance of the sort of thing Hobbes had in mind is quoted from a contemporary source by A. S. P. Woodhouse: 'On Saturday the two politic pulpit-drivers of Independency, by name Nye and Goodwin, were at the debate of settling the kingdom, in the mechanic council at White-hall, and one main question was concerning the extent of magistracy, which Nye and Goodwin requested them not to determine before advice had with some learned divines. Which saying of theirs turned the debate

enthusiast may believe that he has heard God's voice, but it is more likely that he has had a peculiar dream as a result of indigestion or some such local cause.

More important for our present purpose than the role of the heart in the generation of phantasms is its role in the generation of *feelings*. Unlike phantasms, feelings 'seem to be within'. Therefore, the sense of pleasure and pain proceeds

> not from the reaction of the heart outwards, but from continual action . . . towards the heart. For the original of life being in the heart, that motion in the sentient, which is propagated to the heart, must necessarily make some alteration or diversion of vital motion, namely, by quickening or slackening, helping or hindering the same. Now when it helpeth, it is pleasure; and when it hindereth, it is pain, trouble, grief, &c.[1]

'Vital motion', Hobbes immediately explains,

> is the motion of the blood, perpetually circulating (as hath been shown from many infallible signs and marks by Doctor Harvey, the first observer of it) in the veins and arteries.

Thus it is a man's heart which governs his course through life. He calls that 'good' which he desires and that 'evil' which he hates (see below, p. 150); and he desires what helps the circulation of his blood, and hates what hinders it. Hobbes does not, of course, mean that people engage in sex, say, because they consider it good for the circulation. Rather, sex is *intrinsically* pleasurable because of the quickening of vital motion it involves.

Thus man, according to Hobbes's picture of him, is a sort of engine governed by its mainspring or heart. This picture yields various psychological principles, some testable (as we shall see in the next section), some untestable. Among the

---

into a quarrel; for the mechanics took snuff, told them they thought themselves as divine as any divines in the kingdom, which a brother standing by undertook to prove, and pretended a sudden revelation for the purpose . . .' (*Puritanism and Liberty*, p. 127 n.).

[1] *De Corp* IV, xxv, 12 & *EW* i, p. 406.

latter is the principle that men are essentially egocentric. What a man desires is determined by what encourages *his* vital motion; and he can pursue only what he desires: 'of the voluntary acts of every man, the object is some *good to himself*'.[1]

It has occasionally been claimed that Hobbes derived his stark psychological theory from his quasi-mechanistic picture of man. It has also been claimed that he derived it, on the contrary, from his observations of men—more particularly, from his observations of proud and ambitious contemporaries of his, and of his own timorous self. I shall not take up the biographical question concerning what inspired him to develop his psychological theory as he did. I shall consider its logical lay-out. My claim will be that a set of metaphysical ideas about human nature and a set of empirical generalizations about human behaviour both play indispensable roles in his psychological theory, but that it is not derivable from either set alone. Rather, it consists of those empirical generalizations systematically interpreted (or processed or distorted) by those metaphysical ideas.

Consider, by way of illustration, that small part of Hobbes's psychological theory which deals with laughter; it says that laughter is a sort of self-applause.[2] That *men laugh* is not derivable from Hobbes's quasi-mechanistic picture of man which makes no special provision for mirth (machines are not much given to laughing). That *men applaud themselves* when they laugh is hardly derivable from empirical generalizations vouched for by everyday observations: we sometimes observe people apparently laughing at other people's jokes. Hobbes's account of laughter gives the empirical truism that men laugh the distinctive twist demanded by the egocentricity-principle; and this principle, as we have just seen, is yielded by Hobbes's idea that mind is body-dependent and that bodies are heart-governed.

But if people laugh at other people's jokes, is not Hobbes's

[1] *Lev* p. 66 & *EW* iii, p. 120.
[2] p. 27 & p. 46.

claim that laughter is self-applause a *falsified* empirical hypothesis, rather than a claim which puts an unfalsifiable metaphysical interpretation on a true empirical generalization?
Well, your joke may occasion my laughter without exactly
being what I am laughing at: perhaps the delightful thing
about it is that *I* can see its point (if you had had to explain it
to me, I might not have been amused). Like other metaphysical
interpretations, Hobbes's interpretation of laughter says something, but without running any empirical risks. It allows that
my laughter may be externally occasioned, but insists that it
always celebrates something about myself.

Hume seems to have appreciated the unfalsifiable character
of Hobbes's egocentricity-principle:

> A Hobbist readily allows, that there is such a thing as friendship
> in the world, without hypocrisy or disguise, though he may
> attempt, by a philosophical chemistry, to resolve the elements of
> this passion . . . into those of another, and explain every affection
> to be self-love, twisted and moulded, by a particular turn of
> imagination, into a variety of appearances.[1]

Besides laughter and friendship, pity is another human
phenomenon which Hobbes reinterpreted in the same controversial but empirically irrefutable way. One might suppose that
the idea of the fundamental egocentricity of men rules out
the possibility of unhypocritical pity. Hobbes's egocentricity-
principle, however, allows for unhypocritical pity but interprets
it as the product of self-concern plus the imaginary transfer of
oneself into another's shoes.

But here an objection is likely to be raised. For Hobbes's
account of pity is commonly supposed to have been *refuted* by
Bishop Butler;[2] and Butler appealed to well-known *empirical*
facts—for example, to the fact that the sight of a friend in
distress tends to arouse more pity than that of a stranger in

[1] *Enquiries*, pp. 296–7.
[2] See Sermon V in *Works*, ed. Gladstone, 1897, ii, pp. 79 f. C. D. Broad
called Butler's 'refutation' short and annihilating (*Five Types of Ethical
Theory*, 1930, p. 64) and A. E. Taylor spoke of Butler doing 'the work of
refutation so thoroughly . . .' (*Philosophy*, October 1938, p. 407).

similar distress. Thus if Butler's refutation were successful, we
should be incorrect in claiming that Hobbes was imposing upon
uncontroversial generalizations, which cannot be empirically
refuted because they are true, a controversial interpretation
which cannot be empirically refuted because it is metaphysical.

Butler selected for criticism the following statement from
The Elements of Law:

> PITY is imagination or fiction of future calamity to ourselves,
> proceeding from the sense of another man's [present] calamity.[1]

Butler took this to be an eccentric claim about the *word* 'pity'.
His 'refutation' presupposes that Hobbes was propounding a
lexicographical thesis. Now the expression 'pity for another',
in its ordinary significance, obviously does *not* mean 'fear for
oneself'. Butler had no trouble in showing that we get ludicrous
results if we 'substitute [Hobbes's alleged] *definition* instead
of the word *pity*' in typical contexts.

But Hobbes was not arguing about words; he was making a
controversial *factual assertion* about the origin of the familiar
feeling ordinarily called 'pity'. This may not be obvious in
this passage in *The Elements of Law*; but it is obvious in the
corresponding passage in *Leviathan*, which Butler might have
consulted. There, Hobbes begins with a thoroughly uncontroversial definition of the word 'pity', and goes on to explain
how an egocentric human being can yet feel pity for others:

> Grief, for the calamity of another, is PITY; and ariseth from the
> imagination that the like calamity may befall himself.[2]

He adds that such grief is also called 'compassion'. To Butler's
rhetorical question, 'Does not everybody by compassion mean
an affection, the object of which is another in distress?', Hobbes
could have replied: 'That is certainly what *I* mean—and have

---

[1] I, ix, 10 & *EW* iv, p. 44. (The word 'present', added in the Tönnies
edition, was not in the edition from which Butler quoted. Nothing turns
on this.)

[2] p. 27 & *EW* iii, p. 47.

said that I mean—by "compassion"; and I assert that compassion results from self-concern plus imagination of oneself in the other's situation.'

Hobbes explained how other-directed feelings arise from egocentric feelings; he did not explain other-directed feelings away.[1] The ironical thing is that Butler actually *accepts* something like Hobbes's account of pity as manifestly true! His 'refutation' opens with these words:

> There being manifestly this appearance of men's substituting others for themselves, and being carried out and affected towards them as towards themselves; . . .

As we should expect, the facts which Butler cited do not tell against a view so similar to the one which he himself accepted. Hobbes had explained that respectable citizens tend to feel more pity for an innocent victim than for a criminal undergoing punishment because it is easier for them to imagine themselves in the former's shoes. This sort of explanation could readily be extended to cover our tendency to feel more pity for friends than for strangers in equal distress. Nor does Hobbes's account imply that unusually compassionate people are unusually fearful people. Compassion is a function, not of self-concern alone, but of this plus imaginative ability; and Hobbes could have held that unusually compassionate people are people with an unusual capacity for imagining themselves in other people's shoes. Actually, Hobbes's 'atrocious'[2] theory has a rather respectable pedigree: Aristotle had essentially the same idea.[3]

Having extracted two metaphysical principles (uniformity and egocentricity) from Hobbes's mechanistic-cum-biological

---

[1] A fact not appreciated by Sir Leslie Stephen, who declared that Hobbes 'had no difficulty in altogether denying the existence of sympathy' (*Hobbes*, 1904, p. 143).

[2] Leslie Stephen's good-humoured epithet (*op. cit.*, p. 140).

[3] 'Pity may be defined as a feeling of pain caused by the sight of some evil, destructive or painful, which befalls one who does not deserve it, and which we might expect to befall ourselves or some friend of ours, and moreover to befall us soon' (*Rhetoric*, 1385b, 13–16).

account of men, we must go on to draw out some implications of a more predictive character.

§ 22   *Life, death and equality*

One of Hobbes's earliest convictions was that sense-experience results from *alterations* in the internal motions of the body.[1] If we do not normally sense our bones it is because their gentle pressure on sensitive neighbouring membranes hardly varies; and if a sense-organ were subjected to a continuous and unvarying external pressure, no phantasm would result.[2] Again, feelings of pleasure and pain result from *alterations* in the vital motion of the body. One implication of this is that an organism in a state of absolute physical calm would have no phantasms and no feelings:

> there is no such thing as perpetual tranquility of mind, while we live here; because life itself is but motion, and can never be without desire, nor without fear, no more than without sense.[3]

Another implication is that a state of satiety is not pleasurable, since it involves no *enhancing* of vital motion: 'the felicity of this life, consisteth not in the repose of a mind satisfied'.[4] It is, so to speak, accelerations of the vital motion which give off pleasure in the human engine. Felicity is a dynamic rather than a static condition, 'a continual progress of the desire'.[5] Felicity consists 'not in having prospered, but in prospering'.[6]

This physiological theory of pleasure and pain has, furthermore, strong implications about men's evaluation of violent death. We all find the prospect of getting killed distasteful. But would one necessarily find it worse than all alternatives? Might one not prefer to die rather than live painfully?—or to live gloriously for a time, knowing that one will be killed at the end of it, rather than eke out a humdrum existence free from the

---

[1] See G. C. Robertson, *Hobbes*, pp. 33–4.
[2] *De Corp* IV, xxv, 5 & *EW* i, p. 394.
[3] *Lev* pp. 29–30 & *EW* iii, p. 51.   [4] p. 47 & p. 85.   [5] *loc. cit.*
[6] *El of L* I, vii, 7 & *EW* iv, p. 33.

threat of violent death? Hobbes's physiological theory yields negative answers to these two questions.

No-change-in-vital-motion provides the neutral point between pleasure and pain for a Hobbesian pleasure/pain scale; proceeding from this point in a negative direction, vital motion is increasingly hindered and pain increases, until finally vital motion is stopped altogether. Death is located at the negative limit of the scale. Thus a man will regard getting killed as the most *painful* thing which could happen to him:

> Necessity of nature maketh men . . . to avoid that which is hurtful; but most of all that terrible enemy of nature, death, from whom we expect both the loss of all power, *and also the greatest of bodily pains in the losing.*[1]

Hobbes's physiological theory implies that sane men will always prefer to endure pain rather than be killed. If a man kills himself he must be insane.[2]

So there is no pain so bad as the anticipated pain of unnatural death. Is there any condition so desirable that a man would still strive for it even if he knew that the price he will afterwards pay for attaining it is death?

There is an important asymmetry between the two sides of Hobbes's pleasure/pain scale: on the pain side it comes to a natural limit, but on the pleasure side it stretches away indefinitely; there is no fixed limit to the *enhancing* of vital motion.[3] There is an absolutely worst but no absolutely best. Death and pleasure are incommensurable: no amount of pleasure *equals* the pain of death. Aversion to death is not just one of various dispositions which the individual tries to satisfy

---

[1] *El of L* I, xiv, 6 & *EW* iv, p. 83, my italics.

[2] 'For naturally and necessarily the intention of every man aimeth at somewhat which is good to himself, and tendeth to his preservation. And therefore, methinks, if he kill himself, it is to be presumed that he is not *compos mentis*' (*EW* vi, p. 88).

[3] 'There is no such *finis ultimis*, utmost aim, nor *summum bonum*, greatest good, as is spoken of in the books of the old moral philosophers' (*Lev* p. 47 & *EW* iii, p. 85). And see Leo Strauss, *The Political Philosophy of Hobbes*, p. 16.

collectively in an optimum way. It overrides the rest; its demands have priority over all others.

> Every man is desirous of what is good for him and shuns what is evil, but chiefly the chiefest of natural evils, which is death; and this he doth by a certain impulsion of nature, no less than that whereby a stone moves downward.[1]

This idea of men's overriding aversion to being killed, together with the idea that in a state of nature every man is capable of being killed by any other man, yields a key principle in Hobbes's civil philosophy: the principle of natural equality. We have already seen (p. 46 above) that Hobbes's materialism yields the anti-Platonic and anti-Aristotelian principle that there are no *qualitative* differences between men, that men are essentially uniform, having 'one kind of soul, and the same faculties of mind'.[2] And Hobbes further insisted that the brittleness and vulnerability of the human frame is such that, despite quantitative differences of strength and prowess between men, it is in principle easy 'even for the weakest man to kill the strongest'.[3]

It is chastening for a man to admit this natural equality. As a child he had imperiously demanded the satisfaction of his whims; and as a grown man he would still *like* to impose his will on other people.[4] Yet for him to imagine that he is naturally able to do so, in virtue of his superior strength, is a dangerous kind of unrealism. A man in a dangerous situation—as all men in a state of nature are—who underestimates its danger from a proud belief in his own superiority, thereby *increases* the danger. Being life-endangering, such pride is forbidden by a law of nature:

> For the ninth law of nature, I put this, *that every man acknowledge other for his equal by nature.* The breach of this precept is *pride.*[5]

---

[1] *De Cive* i, 7 & *EW* ii, p. 8. [2] *De Corp* I, i, 7 & *EW* i, p. 8.
[3] *De Cive* i, 3 & *EW* ii, p. 6; and see *Lev* p. 60 & *EW* iii, p. 110.
[4] *EW* vii, p. 73. [5] *Lev* p. 77 & *EW* iii, p. 141.

We can agree with Strauss that for Hobbes pride, in the sense of a vain belief in one's superior power, was a main source of evil (see above, p. 31). According to Hobbes, wickedness results when grown men try to satisfy their natural appetites (which are not wicked in themselves—see below, p. 151) in a childishly unrealistic way: 'a wicked men is almost the same thing with a child grown strong and sturdy'.[1]

― Hobbes's death-aversion principle requires some adjustment to accommodate situations where there is only a *risk* of death; for undoubtedly some people do things—volunteer for military service in time of war, for instance[2]—knowing that they are thereby risking their lives. Hobbes allows, rather casually, that the risk of death may be preferred to the certainty of a lesser pain.[3]

― It might seem that this modification renders Hobbes's death-aversion principle too weak for his purpose; for while it may be well-nigh certain that many men will get killed in a state of nature, does not any particular man at any particular time face only a risk of getting killed? And if he suffers from '*tyrannophobia*, or fear of being strongly governed',[4] may he not prefer that risk to the prospect of life under a harsh sovereign?

Well, life under a sovereign *may* prove miserable, but life (while it lasts) in a state of nature *is* miserable; and while the

---

[1] *De Cive* Pref. & *EW* ii, p. xvii.

[2] See *Lev* p. 112 & *EW* iii, p. 205.

[3] For instance, he remarks that 'most men choose rather to hazard their life, than not to be revenged' (*Lev* p. 76 & *EW* iii, p. 140). In *De Cive* he had incidentally remarked that 'most men would rather *lose* their lives . . . than suffer slander' (iii, 12 & *EW* ii, p. 38, my italics), and that 'a son will rather die, than live infamous and hated of all the world' (vi, 13 & p. 83). It seems to me, however, that these asides should be set aside: they conflict with the emphatic declaration in *De Cive*, quoted on p. 117 above, about men shunning death as a stone moves downward; the second was not repeated in *Leviathan*, while the first was toned down to become the statement just quoted about preferring to *hazard* their lives. I ought to add, however, that both Warrender (*The Political Philosophy of Hobbes*, p. 219) and Oakeshott (*Rationalism in Politics*, pp. 290 f.) would dispute my handling of these two remarks.

[4] *Lev* p. 171 & *EW* iii, p. 316.

probability that a particular man in it will get killed tomorrow may not be very high, the probability that he will eventually get killed if he remains in it approaches certainty. In the jungle animals hardly ever die from old age; and Hobbes claims that

> in this [natural] state . . . it were to be accounted a miracle, if any, even the most strong, should close up his life with many years and old age.[1]

On a long-term view, a state of nature 'certainly is much worse than any subjection whatsoever'.[2]

Thus Hobbes's idea that the mind is body-dependent and the body heart-centred has implications which overcome the barrier set up by the privacy-thesis. Admittedly, other men's thoughts and feelings are hidden from Hobbes; admittedly, Hobbes cannot infer from his enjoyment of the lute that other men enjoy it too: 'I cannot enter into other men's thoughts further than I am led by the consideration of human nature in general'.[3] But a consideration of human nature in general can provide just the essential inside knowledge of men which Hobbes needs for his civil philosophy (and which the sovereign also needs for ruling his subjects); men are restless egocentrics whose desires for self-advancement would generate something approaching the maximum amount of conflict in a state of nature; in such a state, each individual would face the near-certainty of eventually getting killed; but their desire not to be killed is stronger than all their other desires; so, when men in such a situation came to appraise it realistically—to recognize their basic equality and to acknowledge the futility of each trying to dominate the others—they would unanimously decide to try to extricate themselves from it.

---

[1] *De Cive* i, 13 & *EW* ii, p. 12.
[2] vii, 4 & p. 96; and see *Lev* p. 94 & *EW* iii, p. 170.
[3] *EW* vi, p. 200.

VII
Liberty

According to Hobbes, then, what a man primarily demands from civil society is protection; and he is willing to pay for this by forgoing whatever liberty it costs. But, of course, he would like to buy protection as cheaply as possible. Liberty is not his chief political desideratum, but it is *a* desideratum. So we must now consider what idea of liberty Hobbes could, and did, accommodate within his determinist and mechanist theory of human nature. Then, punishment being an infringement of liberty, we will consider what idea of punishment he could accommodate.

§ 23   *Liberty in a causal setting*
One negative point is obvious: whatever liberty may be, it cannot, for Hobbes, involve any interruption of causal processes, any genuine spontaneity; a man's will cannot be self-determining:

> Nothing taketh beginning from itself, but from the action of some other immediate agent without itself. . . . Therefore, when first a man hath an appetite or will to something, to which immediately before he had no appetite nor will, the cause of his will, is not the will itself, but something else not in his own disposing.[1]

Liberty must be so conceived as to be consistent with causal necessity.[2]

---

[1] *EW* iv, p. 274.   [2] See e.g. *Lev* p. 108 & *EW* iii, pp. 197–8.

If Hobbes were to tie his concept of liberty down to his fundamental ideas, he had to tie it to his ideas of *motion*. As a first approximation he suggested a very simple connection:

LIBERTY, or FREEDOM, signifieth, properly, the absence of opposition; (by opposition, I mean external impediments of motion;) and may be applied no less to irrational, and inanimate creatures, than to rational.[1]

But this needed qualifying before it applied to human liberty. It says that a stone is free while rolling down a mountain; and as it stands, it also says that a mountaineer is free who is rolling (involuntarily) down a mountain. Absence of external impediments to *voluntary* motion is what Hobbes took human liberty to be:

A FREEMAN, *is he, that in those things, which by his strength and wit he is able to do, is not hindered to do what he has a will to do.*[2]

So far, so good: a man whose voluntary movement is unimpeded is free; a man whose movement is involuntary is not free. But what physical justification could Hobbes give for this crucial distinction between voluntary and involuntary movement? A man who is moving voluntarily is a physical system whose movements have been predetermined by causal lines stretching away indefinitely, backwards and outwards, from his present behaviour. And so is a man who is moving involuntarily. We ordinarily tend to regard voluntary movement as in some sense guided by something non-physical—by an aim, policy, or intention. We regard the kick of a footballer scoring a penalty goal, unlike a patient's involuntary knee-jerk, as voluntary because controlled. How can such a distinction be drawn by a materialist who regards all kinds of muscular movement as determined by nothing but physical causes? Indeed, can a materialist even admit the existence of anything so intangible as aims, intentions, etc.?

Hobbes's theory of voluntary movement is a most interesting and original answer to such questions. Yet no part of his

[1] *Lev* p. 107 & *EW* iii, p. 196.   [2] p. 108 & pp. 196–7.

system has been so undervalued. This may be partly because a really sharp statement of the theory was difficult without the concepts of the differential calculus, of which Hobbes had only certain anticipatory glimmerings. But the main reason for the relative neglect of his theory is that Hobbes signally failed to advertise its importance. He developed it at a time when a major concern of European philosophers was to find some solution for the formidable problems raised by Descartes' mind/body dualism. Had Hobbes presented it, as he could justifiably have done, as a solution of Descartes' problems, it would surely have been eagerly examined then, and historians of philosophy would have attended to it subsequently. Unfortunately, after Descartes' cold reception of the 'Objections' which Hobbes wrote in 1640 to the *Meditations*, Hobbes ignored Descartes, in his published writings, almost completely for the next twenty years.[1] Hobbes seems to have considered Descartes' idea that the soul is an immaterial thinking substance which inhabits the body as so absurd (see above, p. 44) that it scarcely needed answering. One result of his scornful dismissal of Descartes' immaterialist account of mind was that Hobbes's materialist account was, usually, scornfully dismissed in turn, on the mistaken supposition that he had merely evaded the problem by crassly rejecting one side of Descartes' mind/body dichotomy. In fact, Hobbes *overcame* that dichotomy in a very interesting way.

There was one young man who did perceive the importance of Hobbes's theory. Leibniz, as I shall show, took it up and subsequently developed it into his monadological theory of matter—which is, at bottom, an inverted version of Hobbes's materialist theory of mind. Leibniz's theory was not neglected;

[1] I have found only one reference to Descartes during this period: an approving mention of the latter's explanation of the rainbow (*De Corp* IV, xxvii, 14 & *EW* i, p. 463). The causes of the hostility between the two men are unravelled in F. Brandt's *Thomas Hobbes' Mechanical Conception of Nature*, ch. iv. In his last years Hobbes's attitude softened: there are friendly references to 'Monsieur Des Cartes, a very ingenious man' in the *Decameron Physiologicum*, published when Hobbes was ninety (see e.g. *EW* vii, p. 136).

Leibniz did, of course, have the benefit of the calculus (in his case, it was the *integral* calculus which was of most assistance); and Leibniz did explicitly relate his theory to Descartes' ideas and problems. I shall, therefore, use Leibniz to illuminate Hobbes. My programme will be this. The key concept with which Hobbes overcame the body/mind dichotomy was his concept of *endeavour* (or *conatus*). I shall first consider only the physical significance of this Hobbesian concept. Then (in § 24) I shall examine Leibniz's development of it, and the use he made of it in his attack on Descartes' problems. In the light of this I shall (in §25) examine the psychological significance of Hobbes's endeavour-concept, showing how it enabled him to distinguish between voluntary and involuntary motion, and to provide a psycho-physical basis for his concept of liberty.

I begin with this definition of Hobbes's:

> I define ENDEAVOUR *to be . . . motion made through the length of a point, and in an instant or point of time.*[1]

This appears to equate 'endeavour' with instantaneous speed. Suppose we want an expression for the speed, at any given instant, of a body whose speed is changing. Let it, at that instant, have travelled a distance s during a time t. During the next small time-interval δt it will travel δs at an average speed of $\dfrac{\delta s}{\delta t}$. As δt and δs diminish, the value of $\dfrac{\delta s}{\delta t}$ will tend to a definite limit, which may be designated by '$\dfrac{ds}{dt}$'. This expression represents the speed of the body at an instant. Nowadays, we

---

[1] *De Corp* III, xv, 2 & *EW* i, p. 206. For an illuminating discussion of Hobbes's endeavour-concept, see F. Brandt, *op. cit.*, pp. 294–316. Yet Brandt did not appreciate its significance for the body-mind problem. He asked wonderingly how Hobbes could 'quite calmly identify the psychical with matter and motion' (p. 355). My answer is: by means of his endeavour-concept—which Brandt overlooked at the very place where its philosophical interest is greatest.

are careful not to regard this as a fraction. But it often was regarded as a fraction, as a vanishingly small distance ('the length of a point', to use Hobbes's phrase) divided by a vanishingly small time ('an instant or point of time').

However, Hobbes's definition of 'endeavour' does not do full justice to his idea. He defined 'velocity' as the *power* by which a body moves at its present speed.[1] And it becomes clear that by 'endeavour' he meant, not instantaneous speed, but instantaneous velocity in his sense—the pressure or motive force behind the movement, rather than the movement itself.[2]

There is another complication. So far, we have considered a moving body as having, at any instant, *one* endeavour, corresponding to its motion. But Hobbes saw that its motion might be regarded as the resultant of several endeavours. He speaks of a 'concourse' of 'movents', and indicates that a single endeavour corresponds, not necessarily with the body's actual motion, but with the motion it would have if it had no other endeavours: a stone twirled round in a sling has, among others, a tangential endeavour, but it will fly off at a tangent only if its centripetal endeavour ceases.[3] This complication is important: it opens up a metaphysical theory of matter. Had Hobbes postulated just one endeavour corresponding to a body's actual motion, he would merely have introduced an *ad hoc* duplication. But the idea that its motion may be the resultant of various endeavours prepared the way for a 'haunted-universe' doctrine whereby the physical world is filled by an invisible system of endeavours, powers, pressures, or forces. Even the most dead-seeming chunk of inert matter is, one might almost say, brought to life by this idea, transformed into something humming silently with incipient motion.

Now let us see what Leibniz did with Hobbes's endeavour-concept.

---

[1] *De Corp* III, xv, 1 & *EW* i, pp. 204–5.
[2] See e.g. III, xxii, 1 & p. 333.   [3] See III, xv, 6 & pp. 215–16.

§ 24 *Endeavours and monads*

It is well known that the young Leibniz greatly admired Hobbes (as is clear from a long letter which Leibniz, then twenty-five, wrote in 1670 to Hobbes, then eighty-three).[1] And the possibility that Leibniz's mature philosophy was significantly indebted to Hobbes's has naturally been investigated. Tönnies, the great Hobbes scholar, claimed that the fundamental idea of Leibniz's *De Arte Combinatoria*, and indeed the general plan of the Universal Characteristic, were due to Hobbes.[2] Couturat, the great Leibniz scholar, opposed these claims.[3] Tönnies also claimed that Hobbes's mechanism and nominalism greatly influenced Leibniz. I shall now contend that Leibniz's fundamental idea, the idea that the world is a concourse of *monads*, was derived from Hobbes. In what follows it should be remembered that in the English translation of *De Corpore* the word 'endeavour' corresponds to the word 'conatus' in the Latin original.

A year after his letter to Hobbes (in which Leibniz uses the term 'conatus' in Hobbes's sense), Leibniz wrote a paper entitled 'Theory of Abstract Motion',[4] in which Hobbes's influence is manifest, and which already contains, in a rudimentary form, some of the key ideas of Leibniz's monadology. Here, Leibniz affirms the real existence of indivisibles or *unextended beings*, considered as the 'rudiments' or 'beginnings' of continuous or extended things; thus a line, or a stretch of time, is an infinite aggregate of points or instants; and a finite physical movement is an infinite aggregate of conatuses. Leibniz follows Hobbes closely in his account of conatus. For instance he says

[1] *PPL* i, pp. 162–6 & *G* vii, pp. 572–4.

[2] F. Tönnies, 'Leibniz und Hobbes', *Philosophische Monatshefte*, xxiii, 1887, pp. 557–73; and see G. C. Robertson, 'Leibniz and Hobbes', *Mind*, 1888, pp. 312–14.

[3] L. Couturat, *La Logique de Leibniz*, 1901, app. ii, 'Leibniz et Hobbes', pp. 457–72.

[4] *PPL* i, pp. 217–22 & *G* iv, pp. 221–40. This paper contains what I believe to be his first mention of the principle of sufficient reason (p. 222 & p. 232).

that 'conatus is to motion as a point to space' and that it is the 'beginning' of motion. He also shares Hobbes's idea that conatus is not just a measure of instantaneous speed, but is rather a pressure or force causing movement, and that the overall movement of a body may be the resultant of a plurality of conatuses: there can, Leibniz says, 'be many contrary conatuses in the same body at the same time'.

We have already noticed Hobbes's idea that any motion (however small) propagates a disturbance throughout the universe (see p. 22 above). Hobbes carried this idea over into his account of endeavour: the pressures behind motion are likewise propagated through the universe:

> All endeavour, whether strong or weak, is propagated to infinite distance.[1]

Leibniz writes in a similar vein:

> *Whatever moves*, no matter how feeble, and no matter how large may be the obstacle it meets, *will propagate its conatus in full against all obstructions* into infinity, and furthermore it will impress its conatus on all the rest.[2]

Hobbes had written:

> As a point may be compared with a point, so one endeavour may be compared with another endeavour, and one may be found to be greater or less than another.[3]

And Leibniz wrote:

[1] *De Corp* III, xv, 7 & *EW* i, p. 216.

[2] *PPL* i, p. 218 & *G* iv, p. 229, his italics. This eventually evolved into his idea that each monad mirrors the whole universe from its point of view. The intermediate step was the idea that to every change, however small, in a person's body there corresponds a certain perception, however faint: '. . . So our body must be affected in some way by the changes of all the rest. Now to all the motions of our body there correspond certain perceptions or thoughts of our soul, more or less confused; *thus the soul will also have some thought of all the motions of the universe . . .*' (*PPL* i, pp. 521–2 & *G* ii, pp. 112–13, my italics).

[3] *De Corp* III, xv, 2 & *EW* i, p. 206.

One point is greater than another point, one conatus is greater than another conatus, but *every instant is equal to every other one.*[1]

Leibniz's justification for this was as follows: in a given time-interval the distance traversed by a faster body will be greater than that traversed by a slower body, however small the time-interval: so, if the time-interval becomes vanishingly small—an instant—the *point* traversed by the faster one will still be greater than the point traversed by the slower one.[2]

Now I come to what is, for my present purpose, the most interesting statement in this early paper by Leibniz. He says that the idea of conatus 'opens the door to *the true distinction between body and mind,* which no one has explained heretofore'.[3] Later in the same year (1671) Leibniz, in a letter to Arnauld, after summarizing the conclusions of his 'Theory of Abstract Motion', continued:

From these propositions I reaped a great harvest, not merely in proving the laws of motion, *but also in the doctrine of mind.* For I demonstrated that the true locus of our mind is a certain point or centre. . . . *Thought consists in conation,* as body consists in motion.[4]

So far as I know, it was with these statements in 1671 that Leibniz first broached the idea that mind and matter are not two separate substances, but that the relation between them is analogous to that between an infinitesimal and the finite whole composed by an infinite sum of infinitesimals.

An awkward-looking implication of the idea that a conatus is something psychical, as well as the 'beginning' of something

[1] *PPL* i, p. 220 & *G* iv, p. 230, his italics.

[2] Thirty years later Leibniz, equipped now with his law of continuity, gave a more elegant argument for the idea that one point may have a greater magnitude than another in his 'Justification of the Infinitesimal Calculus by that of Ordinary Algebra' (*PPL* ii, pp. 885–7). (Incidentally, he assumed that if $x = y$, then $\dfrac{x}{y} = 1$ even if $x = y = 0$.)

[3] *PPL* i, p. 220 & *G* iv, p. 230, my italics.

[4] *PPL* i, p. 231 & *G* i, pp. 72–3, my italics.

physical, is that there is something psychical in all moving bodies and, indeed, in all stationary bodies too, since their zero-movement is the result of mutually opposed conatuses. Leibniz accepted this implication, and he handled it in the same way that Hobbes had handled it. Hobbes had conceded that inanimate bodies may possibly have momentary phantasms; but, he added, they have no memory, and memory is indispensable for sense-experience as we understand it.[1] And Leibniz, in that letter to Arnauld, went on to say: 'Every body can be understood as a momentaneous mind, or mind without recollection.'[2]

When Leibniz wrote this he had not yet invented his differential and integral calculus: that came some four years later. I now turn from his youthful affair with Hobbes's endeavour-concept to his mature criticism of Descartes.[3]

According to Descartes, mind is utterly unlike body: 'there is nothing included in the concept of body that belongs to the mind; and nothing in that of mind that belongs to the body'.[4] A body is an extended (or three-dimensional) thing which does not think; a mind is a thinking thing which is not extended. Nevertheless, Descartes claimed that there is interaction between mind and body: he rejected as false the supposition 'that if the soul and the body are two substances of diverse nature, that prevents them from being capable of acting on one another'.[5] But it seemed clear to his contemporaries that Descartes had deceived himself, here. If, as Descartes insisted, a body's state can be altered only by contact with other bodies,[6]

---

[1] *De Corp* IV, xxv, 5 & *EW* i, p. 393.

[2] Leibniz, *loc. cit.* (This foreshadows his idea of unconscious perception.) Tönnies drew attention to this parallel.

[3] For many years Popper has lectured on the development of theories of matter from Parmenides, via Descartes, Leibniz, Kant and Boscovic, to Faraday, Maxwell, Einstein and Schroedinger. Leibniz's criticisms of Descartes are a turning-point in the story, as Popper tells it. (See K. R. Popper, 'Philosophy and Physics', *Proc. XIIth Int. Cong. of Philosophy* (1958), Firenze 1960, vol. ii, pp. 367–74.) Although my account will be given largely in Leibniz's words, it is essentially indebted to Popper.

[4] *PW* ii, p. 101.   [5] *PW* ii, p. 132.   [6] *Principes* II, 37.

how can a person's body be affected by his mind? 'So far as we can know from his writings,' Leibniz commented, 'Descartes gave up the struggle over this problem.'[1] Moreover, not only body-mind interaction but interaction between *bodies* was, according to Leibniz, rendered inexplicable by Descartes' system:

> Important philosophers having attributed the essence of matter only to extension, there has resulted a notion of bodies, previously unheard of, which fails to do justice to . . . the phenomena of nature. . . . For it can be demonstrated that extension without the addition of other qualities is not capable of either action or its passive reception; that everything becomes fluid in the most extreme way, that is, becomes vacuous; that then the cohesion of bodies and what is felt as solid in them cannot be explained. . . .[2]

That the parts of a thing tend to cohere, so that it resists penetration by other bodies, was not at all explained by Descartes' merely geometrical account of matter as essentially extended in three dimensions.

Nor was it explained by atomism, which Descartes rejected. As early as 1669, when he was twenty-three, Leibniz argued that the atomists' explanation of the cohesion of bodies involved a hopeless regress. The atomists

> asserted that the whole cause of cohesion in bodies may be explained naturally through the interweaving of certain shapes such as hooks. . . . But these interlocking instruments themselves must be hard and tenacious in order to do their work of holding together the parts of bodies. Whence this tenacity? Must we assume hooks on hooks to infinity? Yet whatever reason there is for questioning this in the first case will exist also in the second and third, and so without end.[3]

---

[1] *PPL* ii, p. 746 & *G* iv, p. 483.

[2] *Leibniz: Selections*, ed. P. P. Wiener, 1951, pp. 62–3; and see pp. 102 f.

[3] *PPL* i, pp. 172–3 & *G* iv, p. 108. Popper has re-stated Leibniz's argument very clearly: 'Leibniz rejected atoms (which he had believed in when young). For atoms, at the time, were nothing but very small bodies, . . . very small *extensions*. The problem of their extension and impenetrability was precisely the same for atoms as for larger bodies: extended atoms could not help to explain extension, the most fundamental of all the properties of matter' (*op. cit.*, pp. 368–9).

E

Seven years later, in 1676, soon after he had worked out his notation for the integral and differential calculus, Leibniz suggested, in an unpublished note, 'that perfectly fluid matter is nothing but a multitude of infinitely small points or of bodies less than any assignable ones', and that, since solid matter is liquefiable, all matter 'is composed of points'.[1] To someone searching, as Leibniz was, for the indestructible substance(s) which persist(s) through all physical changes, the idea that the physical world is composed out of *points* of some kind has this important advantage over the atomic hypothesis: as we saw, the atomists could give no reason for the alleged physical indivisibility of their atoms; but points are necessarily indivisible.

But what character was Leibniz to attribute to these points? One negative answer is clear: he could not conceive them merely as vanishingly small areas or volumes, for an infinite aggregate of geometrical points would merely yield, once more, 'vacuous' Cartesian matter.

As a way of introducing the positive answer, let us proceed to Leibniz's refutation, in 1686, of Descartes' fundamental principle of the conservation of momentum (mv or mass times velocity). Leibniz showed, with the help of Galileo's law of falling bodies, that this principle of Descartes has the absurd implication that more work can be got out of a machine than is put into it, so that a perpetual motion machine could easily be constructed.[2] He concluded that what is conserved is *force* $\left(\dfrac{mv^2}{2}\right)$; and that which is conserved through all changes is, precisely, the stuff or substance of which the world is made: 'the substance of things itself consists in the force of acting and being acted upon'.[3]

> There is something prior to extension, namely, a natural *force* . . . a conatus or effort which has its full effect unless impeded by a contrary conatus. . . . This force . . . must constitute the inmost nature of bodies. . . .[4]

[1] *PPL* i, pp. 244–5.
[2] *PPL* i, pp. 455–63; and see *PPL* ii, pp. 648–51 and 725–7.
[3] *PPL* ii, p. 815 & *G* iv, p. 508.   [4] *PPL* ii, p. 712.

The points out of which bodies are composed are the loci of forces.

> *Material atoms* are contrary to reason. . . . There are only *substantial atoms*, that is to say, real unities absolutely destitute of parts, which are the sources of action and the absolute first principles out of which things are compounded. . . . One could call them *metaphysical points*.[1]

Later, Leibniz said that such a conatus or 'primitive motive force' is 'what I call a monad'.[2]

As we saw, from the time of his Hobbesian paper on abstract motion in 1671, Leibniz believed that the idea of conatus would yield a solution of the Cartesian body-mind problem; for it suggested a way of overcoming Descartes' absolute dichotomy between matter and mind. A conatus is a physical magnitude, but it is not extended. It is an intensity,[3] and it has a direction. Now feelings and appetites are intensities, and they usually have an orientation. In Leibniz's concept of force, the physical and the psychical merge:

> Matter . . . is but a collection or aggregate of parts to infinity. Now a multitude can derive its reality only from *true unities*. . . . To find these *real unities*, I was obliged to have recourse to a *point real and animated*, so to speak, or to a substantial atom . . . I found that their nature consists of force, which involves something analogous to feeling (*sentiment*) and appetite; and that therefore it was necessary to conceive them in imitation of the notion we have of *souls*.[4]

One might say that Leibniz integrated matter from psychophysical intensities, whereas Hobbes differentiated motion

---

[1] *PPL* ii, p. 745 & *G* iv, p. 482.   [2] p. 818 & p. 511.

[3] Popper has often emphasized the importance of this for the body-mind problem. 'Being an intensity attached to a point, a force may be compared to, say, the steepness of a curve at a point, that is, to a "differential" . . .; and being unextended intensities, forces cannot be "material", in the Cartesian sense' (*Proc. XIIth Int. Cong. Phil.*, ii, p. 369).

[4] *PPL* ii, p. 741 & *G* iv, pp. 478–9. (I have considerably modified Loemker's translation, which is rather misleading here.)

into psycho-physical intensities. To Hobbes we must now return.

§ 25 *Liberty as unimpeded endeavour*

When Hobbes first introduced his endeavour-concept, in *The Elements of Law*, it was in a psycho-physiological context. Previously, in the *Tract*, he had said that desire or appetite 'is a motion of the animal spirits towards the object that moveth them' (see above, p. 45). Now he refined this: appetite consists, not necessarily of an actual movement towards the object, but of a *tendency* to move towards it.

This solicitation is the endeavour or internal beginning of animal motion, which when the object delighteth, is called APPETITE.[1]

In *Leviathan* he spoke of appetites or desires as the 'beginnings of motion' within the human body.

Although unstudied men do not conceive any motion at all to be there, where the thing moved is invisible; or the space it is moved in is, for the shortness of it, insensible; yet that doth not hinder, but that such motions are . . . These small beginnings of motion, within the body of man, before they appear in walking, speaking, striking, and other visible actions, are commonly called EN-DEAVOUR.

This endeavour, when it is toward something which causes it, is called APPETITE, or DESIRE.[2]

Hobbes could have argued along the following lines that his endeavour-theory of desire has the great merit of providing a solution for the Cartesian body-mind problem: 'Descartes was right to insist that thoughts, desires, etc., are not extended. He was also right to insist that material objects are extended. And it does indeed follow that thoughts and desires are not material

[1] *El of L* I, vii, 2 & *EW* iv, p. 31; and see F. Brandt, *Thomas Hobbes' Mechanical Conception of Nature*, p. 301.

[2] *Lev* p. 23 & *EW* iii, p. 39. The idea that fear is incipient flight, anger incipient attack, etc., has often been revived since. See, for example, Stuart Hampshire's inaugural lecture, *Feeling and Expression* (1961).

objects. But it does *not* follow that thoughts and desires are essentially immaterial, or non-physical. By no means all the properties of an extended body have an extensional character. For example, a moving body has, at each instant, a certain speed. Its instantaneous speed is as much a physical property of it as its volume or its weight. But instantaneous speed is not an extensional property: it is a point divided by an instant. And those instantaneous forces which I call 'endeavours' are likewise non-extensional physical magnitudes.

'Descartes got into a hopeless difficulty by erroneously concluding that, since thoughts and desires are not extended, they must be modifications of some immaterial thinking substance. We can form no conception of such a substance;[1] and if, *per impossibile*, we could, we still could not conceive how such a substance could move the body it is supposed to inhabit. But the fact that a man's desires often result in bodily movement ceases to be unintelligible if we understand a desire to be a special kind of endeavour. An endeavour is a tendency to move in a certain direction; and so is a desire. An endeavour results in movement unless it is checked by contrary endeavours; and desire for an object results in movement towards the object unless checked by contrary desires or external impediments. A desire is unextended; and so is an endeavour. A desire may be strong or weak; and so may an endeavour. A man is not a machine inside which an angel is trapped.[2] He is a unitary system which, like other physical systems, has extensional and also non-extensional properties.'

We can now answer the question posed at the beginning of this chapter about what physical justification Hobbes could provide for the distinction between voluntary and involuntary movement. An object in a man's environment may cause a heightening, or lowering, of his vital motion, resulting in an endeavour in him towards, or away from, the object. An endeavour may be smothered by countervailing endeavours; but

[1] See above, p. 44.
[2] See C. D. Broad, *Ethics and the History of Philosophy*, 1952, pp. ix–x and 167.

there will be a predominant, or resultant, endeavour which, environment permitting, will be amplified into large-scale bodily motion. Such motion, and only such motion, is voluntary; and a man is free while his voluntary motion is not hindered by external impediments.

'External impediment' is to be understood quite literally as an impediment outside the man's body. Impediments to voluntary motion within his body reduce his power but not his liberty. A man 'fastened to his bed by sickness' is not thereby deprived of his liberty;[1] and a lame man is not unfree 'because the impediment is in himself'.[2]

A politically significant implication of this concept of liberty is that there is no loss of liberty in obeying a command from *fear* of the consequences of disobeying it. A man's liberty is reduced if something external opposes his endeavour-initiated behaviour, but not if something external *alters the endeavour itself* without opposing the behaviour initiated by his new endeavour.

> For impediment or hinderance signifieth an opposition to endeavour. And therefore if a man be necessitated by extrinsical causes not to endeavour an action, those causes do not oppose his endeavour to do it, because he has no such endeavour to be opposed; and consequently extrinsical causes that take away endeavour, are not to be called impediments.[3]

This means that 'subjects are free, who are not fettered and imprisoned'.[4] Even someone who is voluntarily obeying a gunman is free, for he is not being hindered from doing what he (now) has a will to do, which is to avoid being shot. On this view, laws do not take away liberty, provided they are simple enough and few enough to be easily known and remembered, so that we do not land in gaol through inadvertent transgressions of them.[5] (It should be added that Hobbes sometimes uses the term 'liberty' in a different sense, associated with

---

[1] *Lev* p. 107 & *EW* iii, p. 196.   [2] *EW* iv, p. 274.
[3] *EW* v, p. 352.   [4] *De Cive* ix, 9 & *EW* ii, p. 120.
[5] xiii, 15 & p. 179.

'natural right' and contrasted with 'obligation'. In this sense, a man in the state of nature has entire liberty, however constrained his movements may be.)

§ 26   *Punishment*

If all our acts are causally determined, a man who breaks the law is causally necessitated to do so. Then is it just to punish him for something which, given Hobbes's determinist account of human behaviour, he could not help doing? Bishop Bramhall supposed not.[1] Hobbes replied:

> The intention of the law is not to grieve the delinquent, for that which is past and not to be undone; but to make him and others just, that else would not be so, and respecteth not the evil act *past*, but the good to *come*.[2]

But if the magistrate, in questions of punishment, must 'look not at the greatness of the evil past, but the greatness of the good to follow',[3] might it not sometimes be right to 'punish' an innocent person? If the perpetrator of a particularly noxious crime cannot be discovered, may it not be right, on this purely forward-looking view of punishment, to frame someone and to inflict, with much publicity, severe 'punishment' on him in order to deter others from committing similar crimes?

To this Hobbes's answer is that, while the question of punishment should be answered in a utilitarian spirit when it arises, it arises only in connection with men guilty of breaking the law: 'for punishment is only for transgression of the law, and therefore there can be no punishment of the innocent'.[4]

But where does the sovereign's right to punish law-breakers come from? More especially, from where does he get the right (which Hobbes allows him) to inflict the death-penalty in the

---

[1] *Works*, 1842–5, iv, pp. 90–1.   [2] *EW* iv, p. 253.

[3] *Lev* p. 76 & *EW* iii, p. 140.

[4] p. 165 & p. 304. Warrender draws attention to this passage (*The Political Philosophy of Hobbes*, p. 184). Hobbes's point has been developed independently by A. M. Quinton ('On Punishment' in *Philosophy, Politics and Society*, ed. P. Laslett, 1956).

case of serious crimes? His authority comes from the people below (see above, pp. 73–5); and their primary aim, in giving him supreme authority, was to be *protected* from being killed. In the previous century Luther's friend Melanchthon had argued that, since the sovereign obviously does have the right to punish with death—for this is the essential feature of political authority—and since subjects can hardly be supposed to have given him any right to kill them, he must have received it from God.[1] Afterwards, Clarendon used the same argument against Hobbes's quasi-democratic account of the sovereign's authorization: God, by

> putting the sword into the hand of the supreme magistrate, hath qualified and enabled him to execute that justice which is necessary for the peace and preservation of his people. . . . And this sole proposition [accepted by Hobbes], that men cannot dispose of their own lives, hath bin always held as a manifest and undeniable argument, that sovereigns never had, nor can have their power from the people.[2]

Is Hobbes's civil philosophy vulnerable at this point? When he considers 'by what door the right or authority of punishing . . . came in', the first point he makes is that it 'is not grounded on any concession, or gift of the subjects'.[3] Then was Hobbes obliged to concede that, since the sovereign did not receive it from below, he must have received it from above? No; according to Hobbes, he did not *receive* it from anywhere: in the state of nature he, like other men, had the right to kill others; and he, unlike other men, retains this right intact.

When men make a commonwealth, the man who becomes sovereign gives up no part of this right. Each subject renounces the right to defend other subjects against the sovereign and, moreover, agrees to assist the sovereign in exercising his natural right against other subjects who break the law. No man renounces his right to defend himself. Thus

[1] See J. W. Allen, *A History of Political Thought in the Sixteenth Century* (3rd ed., 1951), p. 32.
[2] *Brief View* . . . pp. 40–1.   [3] *Lev* p. 161 & *EW* iii, p. 297.

the right, which the *commonwealth* hath to put a man to death for crimes . . . remains from the first right of *nature*, which every man hath to preserve himself.[1]

And a subject's right to resist the death-penalty likewise remains from the first right of nature: 'a man cannot lay down the right of resisting them, that assault him by force, to take away his life'.[2] More generally:

The obligation of subjects to the sovereign, is understood to last as long, and no longer, than the power lasteth, by which he is able to protect them.[3]

Hobbes's concept of liberty applies to beasts no less than to men.[4] And much of what he says about human nature applies equally to other animals. He would no doubt have agreed that one tiger is very like another—a powerful engine, causally stimulated, egocentric, restless and instinctively afraid of death. We must now turn to the one great advantage which men have over beasts: their ability to speak.

---

[1] *EW* iv, p. 254. [2] *Lev* p. 66 & *EW* iii, p. 120. [3] p. 114 & p. 208.
[4] 'Such a liberty as is free from necessity, is not to be found in . . . men or beasts. But if by liberty we understand the faculty or power . . . of doing what they will, then certainly that liberty is to be allowed to both' (*De Corp* IV, xxv, 13 & *EW* i, p. 409).

VIII
Language

Having indicated, with his endeavour-concept, how physical motion may give rise to life and appetite, Hobbes needed to indicate how human animals could invent speech, before he went on to show how the endeavours of articulate humans could give rise to civil society; for without speech 'there had been amongst men, neither commonwealth, nor soctiey, nor contract, nor peace, no more than amongst lions, bears, and wolves'.[1] In *The Elements of Law* and in *Leviathan* Hobbes's theory of language makes an early appearance, as one of the indispensable preliminaries to his civil philosophy. This theory —especially in its application to moral language—has important political implications, the chief being that, *pace* Warrender, the sovereign's role *is* to create a public system of moral rules out of a moral vacuum.

§ 27 *Names*

Hobbes rather soft-pedals the Biblical idea that language was a God-given gift to man. He suggests that God only initiated Adam into the naming process, leaving 'him to add more names, as . . . experience . . . should give him occasion'; and in any case, 'all this language gotten, and augmented by Adam and his posterity, was again lost at the Tower of Babel'.[2] Thus

---

[1] *Lev* p. 12 & *EW* iii, p. 18.
[2] p. 12 & pp. 18–19.

post-Babel language, at any rate, is a human invention ('the most noble and profitable invention of all other').

How could human animals invent language out of pre-linguistic materials? Without language, they are without government and society; so Hobbes's answer must start by showing how an individual might invent the rudiments of a private language for himself; and since, for Hobbes, the name is the fundamental linguistic unit, this means that he had first to show how an individual can invent names. His account runs like this.

Like other animals, men tend to regard things associated in experience—cloud and rain, fire and ashes—as signs of one another. It is we who endow them with such significance; nevertheless, these are natural signs, for we do not arbitrarily choose so to endow them. But men are able, in addition, to invent marks and signs which they voluntarily associate with things. It is this ability which raises them 'above the nature of beasts'.[1] In Hobbes's terminology, a *mark* has a mnemonic or memory-jogging significance for its maker, whereas an artificial *sign*—say, a bush outside a wine-merchant's house— has significance for other people as well. All artificial signs are marks, but not all marks are artificial signs. A thing must first be a mark before it can become an artificial sign.[2] Marks are

> sensible things taken at pleasure, that, by the sense of them, such thoughts may be recalled to our mind as are like those thoughts for which we took them.[3]

A mark made by me is, for me, a memory-jogging stand-in for the thing I invented it to remind me of—something like my private 'name' for it, especially if the sensible thing I regularly employ as a mark is a vocal sound. If such a mark somehow became publicly accepted as a sign, it would amount to a *name*:

> A name is a word taken at pleasure to serve for a mark which may raise in our mind a thought like to some thought we had

[1] *El of L* I, v, 1 & *EW* iv, p. 20. [2] *Lev* p. 13 & *EW* iii, pp. 19–20.
[3] *De Corp* I, ii, 1 & *EW* i, p. 14.

before, and which being [disposed in speech and] pronounced to others, may be to them a sign of what thought the speaker had, or had not before in his mind.[1]

A name comes into existence when a certain kind of mark is given a public significance 'by the common consent of them who are of the same language with us (as it were, by a certain contract necessary for human society)'.[2] (It rather looks as though Hobbes, in reconstructing what were really gradual developments as deliberate creations, had made organized society a pre-condition for the creation of language, and a common language a pre-condition for the creation of organized society.)

Thus names are signs which start as marks; marks are designed to recall thoughts; and a name, pronounced to others, is a sign, not of a public thing, but of a thought in the speaker's mind. On a previous occasion I took this to mean that a name is a *name of something in the mind*.[3] But J. M. Brown has since persuaded me that I was wrong.[4] The issue deserves clarification, since names are, for Hobbes, the bricks out of which language is built. I may say that I made this mistake in good company. J. S. Mill, for instance, after asking 'Are names more properly said to be the names of things or of our ideas of things?' remarked: 'The eminent thinker, just quoted [Hobbes], seems to countenance the latter opinion.'[5] And M. J. Oakeshott took Hobbes to mean that names are given to images.[6] I think I can now explain why we were misled.

[1] *De Corp* I, ii, 4 & *EW* i, p. 16. The words in square brackets are missing from the English translation. See G. C. Robertson, *Hobbes'* p. 83 n. Hobbes wrote: '. . . what thought the speaker had, *or had not* before in his mind . . .' to accommodate what he called 'negative' (or 'privative') names: 'by these *negative names*, we . . . signify to others what we have not thought of' (I, ii, 7 & p. 19).

[2] *De Cive* xviii, 4 & *EW* ii, p. 303.

[3] *Philosophical Quarterly*, April 1955, pp. 139–40.

[4] After a correspondence arising from his review (in the *Philosophical Review*, October 1957, pp. 570–2) of R. S. Peters' *Hobbes*; there, Brown charged Peters, and incidentally myself, with a mistake in this connection.

[5] *A System of Logic*, Bk I, ch. ii, § 1. Mill favoured the former opinion.

[6] See his Introduction to *Leviathan* (Blackwell), p. xxiv.

For most people, the words 'Oliver Cromwell' may be said indifferently to *signify*, or *mean*, or *denote*, or *name* the man who became Lord Protector of England in 1653. Now Hobbes said that words *signify* conceptions,[1] that the *meaning* of a word is always a conception of the mind,[2] and that every universal name *denotes* conceptions we have.[3] So most readers tend to conclude that he meant that words *name* conceptions. I thought this a curious doctrine for a nominalist who was also a *materialist* to hold. But I conjectured that he had felt driven to it from a consideration of names of fictional things. I supposed that Hobbes had concluded that, if 'centaur', which is surely a significant word,[4] is not to be excluded as one of those 'names that signify nothing',[5] it must be regarded as signifying or naming something *in the mind*; and that, rather than make an *ad hoc* exception for such names, he had preferred to affirm that *all* names are names of conceptions.

In fact, there was for Hobbes a large difference between what a name signifies and what it names. This was because he identified a name with physical expressions of itself. This is not an identification I would make myself. I prefer to say that if I pronounce or write the words 'Oliver Cromwell' a hundred times, I pronounce or write, not a hundred names, but one name a hundred times, and that it is the self-same name whether pronounced softly or in a high-pitched voice or written in green ink or in capital letters.

But Hobbes's materialism did not allow him to regard a name as an abstract entity immanent in, but not identical with, its various physical expressions. He regarded *each* such expression as a name; and this means that a name cannot be taken as a *sign* of the thing itself—otherwise, my pronouncing 'Oliver Cromwell' would signify Cromwell's presence in the room with me. Rather, this particular name which I have just pronounced signifies the presence in my mind of some idea of Cromwell. On the other hand, Hobbes does remark, briefly

[1] *El of L* I, vi, 3 & *EW* iv, p. 28.   [2] I vi, 4 & p. 28.
[3] *De Corp* I, vi, 11 & *EW* i, p. 80.   [4] *Lev* p. 5 & *EW* iii, p. 6.
[5] p. 20 & p. 34.

and in passing, that names are *names* 'of the things them-selves';[1] and rather than make an *ad hoc* exception for names like 'centaur' he, on the contrary, extended the title of *thing* to feigned entities like centaurs:

> But seeing every name has some relation to that which is named, though that which we name be not always a thing that has a being in nature, yet it is lawful for doctrine's sake to apply the word *thing* to whatsoever we name; as if it were all one whether that thing be truly existent, or only feigned.[2]

I ought not to have overlooked that Hobbes admits a name-thing relation as well as a sign-conception relation. My excuse is that, while he says a great deal about the latter, he says almost nothing about the former. He says almost nothing about the name-thing relation because his materialism and causal psycho-logy did not allow him to describe it. He could and did give a causal account of the way in which a thing may arouse a con-ception of itself in someone's mind. He could and did give a causal account of the way in which someone may signal the presence of a conception in his mind by making a vocal noise. But he did not give a causal account of the relation between the name and the thing(s) it names; and I do not think he could. I follow Popper in believing that a causal account of *this* relation *cannot* be given.[3] Thus although Hobbes mentions the existence of 'some relation' between every name and that which is named by it, he never *characterizes* this relation, but gives instead a roundabout causal account in which it is the sign-conception relation which is prominent. It is this which misled me, and perhaps others, into supposing that he regarded names as the names of our conceptions rather than of the things themselves.

---

[1] *De Corp* I, ii, 6 & *EW* i, p. 17.   [2] I, ii, 6 & p. 18.

[3] See K. R. Popper, *Conjectures and Refutations*, pp. 297–8. Very briefly, Popper's argument is this: imagine a machine which, whenever a certain ginger cat appears in its environment, spells out 'MIKE'. This may look like a causal realization of the thing-name relation, but only because *we* pick out just the cat and 'MIKE' from a continuous physical process which was already under way before the cat appeared and goes on after 'MIKE' has been signalled.

Hobbes divides names into proper names, and common or universal names. The main difference is simply that whereas a (univocal) proper name like 'Charles I of England' names just one thing, a universal name like 'Man' names many things.[1] A universal name is a sort of pluralized version of a proper name. The world contains things but not, according to Hobbes's materialist ontology, any universal things or real essences. The world also contains conceptions or images or ideas of things, but not, according to his sensationalist psychology, any universal ideas:

> They err, that say the *idea of anything is universal*; as if there could be in the mind an image of a man, which were not the image of some one man, but of a man simply, which is impossible; for every idea is one, and of one thing.[2]

There is nothing universal, either outside or inside the mind, for a universal name to name. All things are individual. The only individual things which may properly be called 'universal' are the so-called 'universal' *names* themselves:

> there being nothing in the world universal but names; for the things named are every one of them individual and singular.[3]

With the help of the idea that a single name may be composed of several words each of which is a part of that name,[4] Hobbes was able to regard all sorts of words, with one single exception, as names or parts of names (though some names are of 'indefinite signification'). Thus although 'all' is not itself a name, it is part of, for example, the name 'all men'; 'this' is part of the name 'this man'; and 'some' is part of the (indefinite) name 'some men'.[5] The exception is the copula: 'is', 'are', etc. It is the copula which enables men to string names together to form propositions.[6]

---

[1] *De Corp* I, ii, 9 & *EW* i, pp. 19–20.   [2] I, v, 8 & p. 60.
[3] *Lev* p. 13 & *EW* iii, p. 21.   [4] *De Corp* I, ii, 14 & *EW* i, p. 23.
[5] I, ii, 11 & p. 21.
[6] I, iii, 2 & pp. 30–1. 'But what shall we now say,' Hobbes asked in his fourth objection to Descartes' *Meditations*, 'if reasoning chance to be nothing more than the uniting and stringing together of names or designations by the word *is*?' (*PW* ii, p. 65).

§ 28   *Propositions*

Hobbes held what may be called a Humpty-Dumpty theory of meaning.[1] Did he also hold a Humpty-Dumpty theory of truth—did he believe that the truth or falsity of propositions is determined by human will? Leibniz thought that he did:

> Hobbes seems to me to be a super-nominalist. For not content, like the nominalists, to reduce universals to names, he says that the truth of things itself consists in names and, what is more, that it depends on the human will, because truth allegedly depends on the definitions of terms, and definitions depend on the human will.[2]

In this section I shall argue as follows: had Hobbes consistently abided by his nominalist ontology (that there is nothing universal in the world but names, every thing named being individual and singular), Leibniz would have been right; moreover, Hobbes often appears to endorse the 'super-nominalist' view that the truth or falsity of all propositions is automatically determined by nothing but verbal conventions or stipulations; however, Hobbes did not consistently abide by his nominalist ontology: he sometimes allowed that a common name may stand for something which is *not* individual and singular—for a characteristic or a property or (as he called it) an *accident* which may be shared by many individual things; and the admission of accidents into his ontology enabled him to avoid a Humpty-Dumpty theory of truth, at least in connection with factual propositions. In the section after this I shall argue that, since he did not admit any moral accidents (or non-natural qualities, as G. E. Moore called them), Hobbes did

---

[1] ' "When I use a word," Humpty-Dumpty said in rather a scornful tone, "it means just what I choose it to mean—neither more nor less."
' "The question is," said Alice, "whether you *can* make words mean so many different things."
' "The question is," said Humpty-Dumpty, "which is to be Master—that's all." ' (Lewis Carroll, *Through the Looking-Glass*, ch. vi.)

[2] *PPL* i, p. 199 & *G* iv, p. 158.

perforce take a Humpty-Dumpty view of moral utterances, the role of Humpty-Dumpty being given to the sovereign.

That Hobbes's nominalist ontology *without* the addition of accidents leads to a Humpty-Dumpty theory of truth and falsity can be indicated in the following way. Suppose than an object *a* (an object whose proper name is '*a*') has been given the common name '*G*', that an object *b* has been given the common name 'not-*G*',[1] and that it is now to be decided whether an object *c* should be called *G* or not-*G*. Given a strictly nominalist ontology, could such a decision be regulated, however loosely, by objective considerations? It might be answered: 'Yes; a necessary condition for *c* to be called *G* is that *c* should at least be—to put it roughly—rather like *a* and rather unlike *b*.' The trouble is that it is well-nigh certain that *c* will be rather like *a* and unlike *b* in some respects, and also rather like *b* and unlike *a* in other respects. If *a* is a tiger and *b* is a whale and *c* is a shark, *c* may be rather like *a* and unlike *b* with respect to man-eating tendencies, and rather like *b* and unlike *a* with respect to sea-going tendencies.

Speaking as a non-nominalist, and taking negative and relational properties into account, I believe that any object will have indefinitely many properties in common with any other particular object, however dissimilar. (The piece of paper on which I am writing is like the Tower of Pisa in that it is coloured, was made after the birth of Christ, was not burnt in the Great Fire of London . . .) I also believe that there will be indefinitely many properties possessed by only one of any two objects, however similar. (The new piece of paper on which I am now writing is to the right of the old piece, is slightly nearer the sun, was being written on when our cat woke up . . .) Thus any object both trivially resembles any other object in indefinitely many ways and is trivially different from it in indefinitely many ways. This means that interesting resemblances and interesting differences are always resemblances and differences with respect to selected general features (or charac-

[1] For Hobbes, both 'man' and 'not-man' are names (*De Corp* I, ii, 16 & *EW* i, p. 27).

teristics or properties or accidents). We should never say simply that c is like a and unlike b, or even that c is more like a than b; we should say that c is more like a than b with respect to specified features. Thus a strict nominalist who disallows any appeal to general features, etc., thereby disallows any appeal to likenesses. For him, the decision as to whether c should be called G or not-G cannot be regulated by comparisons between c and a and b. Nor, of course, can it be regulated by considering whether c possesses a property of G-ness. The decision cannot be regulated by objective considerations. Past ascriptions of the common name 'G' do not create precedents governing future ascriptions of it. Whether c is to be G or not will depend on the free decision of the name-giver. Each object must be independently christened.

Suppose that a nominalistic language were built up in this way, each object having one proper name, and selected common names, ascribed to it. How would the truth or falsity of any sentence formulated in this language be determined? The true, and rather devastating, answer to this question was, so far as I know, first given by Popper: 'in a purely nominalistic language no sentence can be formulated whose truth or falsity could not be decided by merely comparing the defining lists, or enumerations, of the things which are mentioned in the sentence.'[1] The sentence 'a is G' is true if and only if the thing to which the proper name 'a' has been ascribed is one of the things to which the common name 'G' has been ascribed; 'Every G is H' is true if and only if every thing named 'G' has also been named 'H'. In such a language, truth and falsity would indeed 'depend on the human will', as Leibniz put it—depend on the unregulated, free decisions of the name-imposers.

Hobbes often wrote as though he embraced just this view of truth and falsity. Consider the following five quotations. (I number them, because I shall be referring to them later.)

[1] K. R. Popper, *Conjectures and Refutations*, p. 262.

(1) A *true* proposition is that . . . whose predicate is the name of every thing, of which the subject is the name.[1]

(2) That proposition only is true, . . . in which are copulated two names of one and the same thing.[2]

(3) The first truths were arbitrarily made by those that first of all imposed names upon things.[3]

(4) Men pronounce *falsely*, by their own negligence, in departing from such appellations of things as are agreed upon.[4]

(5) To *know truth*, is the same as to *remember* that it was made by ourselves by the very usurpation of the words.[5]

Moreover, Hobbes seems to endorse the depressing implications which such a view has for *argument*.[6] Suppose that you, knowing that I say that *a* is *G*, declare that *a* is not-*G*; on this view, the difference between us is not factual; the question is not, which is right but, 'which is to be Master'—whose naming conventions are to prevail. If neither of us is willing to yield to the other we must either appeal to an arbitrator, or fight it out, or continue to differ:

> The parties must by their own accord, set up, for right reason, the reason of some arbitrator, or judge, to whose sentence they will both stand, or their controversy must either come to blows, or be undecided, for want of a right reason constituted by nature; so is it also in all debates of what kind soever.[7]

Since our differences cannot be resolved by rational considerations, an arbitrator's resolution of them will be arbitrary.

Had Hobbes subscribed to a completely conventionalist view of truth, it would have been inconsistent of him to regard explanatory theories in natural philosophy as hypotheses which *may* be true (see above, pp. 69–71). In fact, he did not subscribe to such a view of truth because he did not abide by his nominalist ontology. He not only admitted resemblances between

---

[1] *De Corp* I, iii, 7 & *EW* i, p. 35.   [2] I, v, 2 & p. 57.
[3] I, iii, 8 & p. 36.   [4] I, v, 1 & p. 56.
[5] *De Cive* xviii, 4 & *EW* ii, p. 304.
[6] 'Hobbes treated argument rather like a wrestling bout in which the point was to throw the other fellow and glory in his discomfiture' (R. S. Peters, *Hobbes*, p. 175).   [7] *Lev* p. 19 & *EW* iii, p. 31.

things, but *resemblances with respect to certain properties or accidents*; and he said, in effect, that a common name gets extended to new objects, not arbitrarily, but in accordance with such objective resemblances. There was already a hint of this view in *The Elements of Law*, where he said that universal names are 'called indefinite; because we limit them not ourselves, but leave them to be applied by the hearer'.[1] And in *Leviathan*, immediately after the declaration that there is nothing universal in the world but names, he added: 'one universal name is imposed on many things, *for their similitude in some quality, or other accident*'.[2] In *De Corpore* he spoke of 'that accident for which we give a certain name to any body',[3] having previously included *accidents* among the 'things to which we give names'.[4]

I can see no escape from the conclusion that his statement that some names are names of accidents is inconsistent with his statement that there is nothing universal in the world but names, every thing named being individual and singular.[5] For Hobbes goes out of his way to contrast accidents with individual things: 'bodies are things, and not generated; accidents are generated, and not things'.[6] Nor are accidents parts of things, though they accompany things and cannot exist apart from things.[7] The same accident (hardness, say) can accompany many things, but one thing cannot be in many places at once. Most accidents (figure and extension are exceptional) may be annihilated, but a thing cannot be.[8] A thing may go out of one place into another, but an accident cannot go out of one thing into another.[9] Hobbes's distinction between things and accidents was not drawn by an old man on the defensive: he had already drawn it in the *Tract*.[10]

---

[1] I, v, 6 & *EW* iv, p. 22.   [2] p. 13 & *EW* iii, p. 21, my italics.
[3] II, viii, 23 & *EW* i, p. 117.   [4] I, v, 2 & pp. 57–8.
[5] R. S. Peters offers a defence of Hobbes against this charge (*Hobbes*, pp. 129–32), but I am afraid I did not quite follow it.
[6] *De Corp* II, viii, 20 & *EW* i, p. 117.
[7] I, iii, 3 & p. 33.   [8] II, viii, 3 & p. 104.
[9] II, viii, 21 & p. 117.   [10] See sect. i, concs. 1–4.

In the light of this account of accidents, the five quotations given on p. 147 above may be open to a less conventionalist reading than they at first seemed to call for. The first and second quotations might be conflated and read in this way: 'A [subject-predicate] proposition is true if and only if every thing to which the predicate-name either has already been ascribed or could properly be extended is a thing to which the subject-name either has already been ascribed or could properly be extended.' The third quotation might be read thus: 'The *first* truths (but by no means all subsequent truths) were arbitrarily made by those that first of all imposed names upon things'; suppose that the things on which the name '*H*' was first imposed included all the things on which the name '*G*' had so far been imposed; then 'Some *H* are *G*' would indeed be an arbitrary 'first truth'; but 'All *G* are *H*' could be a contingent hypothesis; for something might turn up to which the name '*G*' was applicable (in virtue of its similarity to the things already called *G*), but to which the name '*H*' was inapplicable (since it lacked the accident in virtue of which things have been called *H*). The fourth quotation might be read thus: 'One way in which men pronounce falsely is by departing from agreed appellations (and they sometimes pronounce falsely when they stick to agreed appellations).' I confess that I do not see how to bring the fifth quotation into line. It, unlike the first four which come from *De Corpore*, comes from a section in *De Cive* where Hobbes was discussing religious faith. His nominalist tendencies were always uppermost in religio-political contexts, as we shall shortly see.

A strict nominalist has considerable difficulty in coping with *changing* things. He interprets common names on the analogy of proper names; and a proper name is not normally replaced when its owner undergoes changes. Then why, if a man called Young does not lose this name when he grows old, should an unripe tomato called green lose this name when it ripens? With the admission of accidents, this ceases to be a problem: the unripe tomato possessed an accident in virtue of which the tomato was called green; but now that it has ripened, that accident has perished and the tomato is no longer called green.[1]

If I am right, Hobbes's starkly nominalist tendencies are off-set, in his account of descriptive names and factual proposi-tions, by tendencies of a more Aristotelian character.[2] In his account of descriptive language it seems that Hobbes's heavy emphasis on the arbitrariness of the initial awards of names to objects is, after all, innocuous: although these initial namings are necessarily arbitrary and automatically engender some conventional truths, they do not make all truths conventional, since names are thereafter extended in (if I may be forgiven a pun) an accident-prone manner. To meet the stark implications of a consistent nominalism we must turn to the moral field, where there is, according to Hobbes, nothing objective to regulate the award of moral names.

§ 29   Moral epithets and utterances

Hobbes's whole theory of moral language is implicit in this famous passage from *Leviathan*:

> But whatsoever is the object of any man's appetite or desire, that is it which he for his part calleth *good*: and the object of his hate and aversion, *evil*; and of his contempt, *vile* and *inconsider-able*. For these words of good, evil, and contemptible, are ever used with relation to the person that useth them: there being nothing simply and absolutely so; nor any common rule of good and evil, to be taken from the nature of the objects themselves; but from the person of the man, where there is no common-wealth; or, in a commonwealth, from the person that represen-teth it. . . .[3]

There are no objective moral properties to regulate the use of moral epithets. Men in a state of nature, who possess moral

[1] *De Corp* II, viii, 20 & *EW* i, p. 116.

[2] Thus at one place he writes: 'Now that accident for which we give a certain name to any body . . . is commonly called the ESSENCE thereof; as rationality is the essence of man' (II, viii, 23 & p. 117).

[3] p. 24 & *EW* iii, p. 41.

language (see above, p. 73), will bandy these epithets about each in accordance with his personal appetites and desires. One implication of this is that, if moralizing talk in the state of nature makes any difference, it *worsens* men's condition. Their interpersonal conflicts are engendered by their personal appetites; and their 'moral' judgements are merely pretentious projections of their appetites. So moralizing talk will tend to make the conflicts more stubborn and bitter. Avowals of an 'I want that' variety will swell into demands of a 'That is rightfully mine' variety.

> All controversies are bred from hence, that the opinions of men differ concerning *meum* and *tuum*, *just* and *unjust*, . . . and the like; which every man esteems according to his own judgement.[1]

A man's natural appetites are not sinful.[2] What is objectionable is his moralized projection of them in the form of pseudocommandments to which other men are vainly expected to submit. This inflates conflicts of interest into ideological hostilities.

> *Good*, and *evil*, are names that signify our appetites and aversions; which in different tempers, customs, and doctrines of men, are different. . . . Nay, the same man, in divers times, differs from himself; and one time praiseth, that is, calleth good, what another time he dispraiseth, and calleth evil: from whence arise disputes, controversies, and at last war.[3]

What is needed, to end warring conflicts, is not moralism but realism (especially about men's equal vulnerability—see pp. 117–18 above).

Hobbes reminded Puritan moralizers again and again that the original sin consisted of a disobedient and presumptuous desire to judge of good and evil.[4]

> The most ancient of all God's commands is (Gen. ii, 17): *Thou shalt not eat of the tree of knowledge of good and evil;* and the most

[1] *De Cive* vi, 9 & *EW* ii, p. 77.   [2] *Lev* p. 62 & *EW* iii, p. 114.
[3] *Lev* pp. 79–80 & *EW* iii, p. 146.
[4] See, for example, p. 216 & p. 397.

ancient of all diabolical temptations (Gen. iii, 5): *Ye shall be as gods, knowing good and evil.*[1]

Moreover, the original sin was committed *in vain*; not only were Adam and Eve thrust out of Paradise, but they 'acquired no new ability to distinguish between [good and evil] aright'.[2]

Hobbes's ethical scepticism and ethical authoritarianism went hand in hand. The state of nature consists of a multitude of humpty-dumpties, each vainly trying to be master by making moral words mean what *he* chooses them to mean. If there are to be moral words with generally accepted meanings, and common moral rules, there must be one Humpty-Dumpty who really is Master and who determines what moral words shall denote:

> Before there was any government, *just* and *unjust* had no being, their nature only being relative to some command: and every action in its own nature is indifferent; that it becomes *just* or *unjust*, proceeds from the right of the magistrate.[3]

Since men need what does not exist by nature, it must be manufactured for them.

If men institute a sovereign who shall, among other things, allocate the names 'good', 'evil', 'right', 'wrong', etc., to specified classes of actions, and if thereafter some of his subjects try to reallocate these names according to their personal desires,

---

[1] *De Cive* xii, 1 & *EW* ii, p. 151.

[2] *Lev* p. 106 & *EW* iii, p. 194.

[3] *De Cive* xii, 1 & *EW* ii, p. 151. A. E. Taylor admitted that this appears to tell against his view that moral principles are made by *God* and are contained in the laws of nature; he countered it with the true assertion that 'the Sovereign does *not* make the antecedent and more important distinction between *equity* and *iniquity*' (*Philosophy*, October 1938, p. 413). But this is neutral between his view that Hobbes's natural laws have a *moral* character, and the view that they are assertoric hypothetical imperatives. 'Iniquity' was Hobbes's name for transgressions of the laws of nature (*EW* vi, p. 26). On either view it is not the sovereign who makes the laws of nature (see above, p. 87); so on either view the sovereign does not make the distinction between equity and iniquity.

they will tend to cause a reversion to a state of nature.[1] Among the 'diseases of a commonwealth' Hobbes put the 'seditious' doctrine that *every private man is judge of good and evil actions*.[2]

> Private men, while they assume to themselves the knowledge of *good* and *evil*, desire to be even as kings; which cannot be with the safety of the commonweal.[3]

The doctrine that *whatsoever a man does against his conscience, is sin*, being 'repugnant to civil society',[4] is itself repugnant to the laws of nature, and therefore iniquitous.

In declaring something to be right, or wrong, a sovereign is not describing it or making a *statement* about it. His declaration is, to use J. L. Austin's word, a 'performative'.[5] Sovereigns

> *make* the things they command just, by commanding them, and those which they forbid, unjust, by forbidding them.[6]

Such a declaration is a legislative act; and 'names imposed by statutes are equivalent to definitions'.[7]

Authoritarian-minded contemporaries of Hobbes, such as Filmer and Bossuet, tried to sanctify any commandment a sovereign might care to issue by regarding him as God's regent on earth; but this suggests that anti-religious commands of an infidel sovereign might be disputable. Hobbes, although he regarded the sovereign as the *people's* representative, was able to go still further. His Humpty-Dumpty theory of public morality has the remarkable (and in his eyes salutary) consequence that it is not only iniquitous but *absurd* to dispute the rightness of the sovereign's commandments[8]—as it would be

---

[1] 'How many rebellions hath this opinion been the cause of, which teacheth that the knowledge whether the commands of kings be just or unjust, belongs to private men' (*De Cive* Pref. & *EW* ii, p. xii).

[2] *Lev* p. 168 & *EW* iii, p. 310.   [3] *De Cive* xii, 1 & *EW* ii, p 151.

[4] *Lev* p. 168 & *EW* iii, p. 311.

[5] See his *How To Do Things With Words*, 1962, pp. 4 f.; and *Philosophical Papers*, 1961, chap. 10.

[6] *De Cive* xii, 1 & *EW* ii, p. 151, my italics.   [7] *EW* vi, p. 88.

[8] Even if he commands his Christian subjects to deny Christ; *Lev* pp. 271 and 330–1 & *EW* iii, pp. 493–4 and 601–2. See below, p. 161, n. 3.

absurd to protest that the baby who, in the popular song, was christened 'Franklin D. Roosevelt Jones' had been *falsely* christened by the clergyman. The clergyman was not describing or misdescribing the baby, not stating truly or falsely that the baby had some affinity with President Roosevelt. He was performing a naming ceremony, and his action *made* the baby Franklin D. Roosevelt Jones. In this respect the clergyman acts like a Hobbesian sovereign and unlike a juryman. Jurymen try to satisfy themselves that the accused *is* guilty before they *declare* him 'Guilty'. But

> the makers of civil laws, are not only declarers, but also *makers* of the justice and injustice of actions.[1]

It is for the sovereign

> to make some common rules for all men, and to declare them publicly, by which every man may know what may be called . . . just, what unjust . . . what good, what evil.[2]

If a citizen says that something is unjustly commanded by law, he is being contradictory as well as seditious—saying that something is not and is called just.[3]

I promised (p. 88 above) to challenge Warrender's view of the sovereign's role. The sovereign, he says,

> is concerned with the fulfilment of validating conditions of obligation, in a system of rights and duties that he does not himself control or create except in the most trivial sense.[4]

> The function of the civil sovereign is not to create moral principles nor even to educate the citizen,[5] but to enforce and interpret law.[6]

---

[1] *Lev* p. 306 & *EW* iii, p. 559, my italics.

[2] *De Cive* vi, 9 & *EW* ii, p. 77.

[3] This conclusion was reinforced by Hobbes's theory of authorization: see below, pp. 160–1. Cudworth protested that Hobbes rendered 'injustice a mere ludicrous thing' (*TIS* iv, p. 202).

[4] *The Political Philosophy of Hobbes*, p. 28.

[5] But Hobbes said: 'every sovereign ought to cause justice to be taught' (*Lev* p. 179 & *EW* iii, p. 329); and see *De Cive* xiii, 9 & *EW* ii, pp. 171–2, where the sovereign is called on to root out perverse doctrines, 'not by commanding, but by teaching'.   [6] p. 143.

How, then, does Warrender deal with the sort of evidence we have been considering? He retreats a little:

> The question of whether the civil sovereign determines what is right and what is wrong for his subjects is not capable of a simple answer. Sometimes Hobbes appears to define the terms 'right' and 'wrong' (though not the terms 'good' and 'evil') as what the civil law enjoins or forbids.[1]

(But Hobbes said: 'What the legislator commands, must be held for *good*, and what he forbids for *evil*.')[2] Warrender allows that, because of their largely differing private moral judgements, men have to give up their right to judge in areas where the civil law operates. But he claims that men share two ethical values which are prior to the sovereign and the civil law:

> Men do not disagree in all things which are to be called good or evil; they agree in regarding salvation or self-preservation as their *summum bonum* and death or ultimate destruction as their *summum malum*, and Hobbes never suggests that these are such because the sovereign has commanded that it shall be so. These two values, therefore, stand outside the ethical field which is determined by the civil law. In fact, it is in terms of these values that Hobbes justifies the subjection of the other ethical values of man to the civil law.[3]

But men do not agree about these 'values', nor are they 'ethical'. In the state of nature, man A will regard the preservation of A as the supreme good and the destruction of A as the supreme evil. And man B will similarly evaluate the preservation and destruction of B. There is a psychological similarity here; but there is no *agreement*: A will *not* agree that the preservation of B is the supreme good; A may very well consider the destruction of B a good thing.[4] A and B will agree, if they are realistic and rational, that the only way for each of them to avoid getting killed is for them and all the others to

---

[1] p. 163.   [2] *De Cive* xii, 1 & *EW* ii, p. 150.   [3] p. 164.
[4] Warrender knows this, of course—see *op. cit.*, p. 274.

institute a sovereign who will impose civil laws upon them; but that will be agreement, not over values, but over common means to their very different, though parallel, ends. And their respective ends can hardly be described as ethical: the aversion each has to getting killed is a self-regarding, biological instinct. Emended in accordance with this, the last sentence of the last quotation from Warrender would read: 'In fact, it is in terms of these egocentric survival instincts that Hobbes justifies the subjection of the ethical valuations of man to the civil law'; and with this I agree.

Here, as elsewhere, Warrender tries to assimilate Hobbes's position to the orthodox tradition of natural law:

> Hobbes is asserting that the political relationship requires the sacrifice of the private conscience over a certain field and the substitution of the public conscience of the sovereign. In this his theory is not peculiar. Any political philosophy except one of sheer anarchy proceeds on the assumption that some rules are necessary and must be enforced by the State.[1]

But this glosses over the novel and essential feature of Hobbes's theory. Plenty of natural lawyers have said that men, to avoid anarchy, must submit to positive laws even if they consider them unjust. But *this* is not Hobbes's position. Within Locke's system, and many others, it is possible for a citizen to hold both that a particular law is bad and that he ought nevertheless to obey it. But Hobbes's system excludes the very *possibility* of a wrong or unjust law. Puritans and others think that there is one distinction between right and wrong, and another between legal and illegal; Hobbes, on the contrary (as we have noticed on p. 96 above), was concerned to conflate notions which, left apart, cause citizens to 'see double'; and his nominalism enabled him to declare 'that no *law* can possibly be *unjust*'.[2] Hobbes's theory *is* peculiar in its nominalist authoritarianism and stark legal positivism—as the attacks on it by natural lawyers testify.[3]

[1] p. 164.   [2] *EW* iv, p. 252.
[3] See, for example, Richard Cumberland, *Laws of Nature* I, iii, 2; II, v, 5; III, ix, 10; III, ix, 20.

What has been said about moral words applies *pari passu* to the terms of religious worship. No words describe God, for he is indescribable. The words we use about him are 'meant not to declare what he is (for that were to circumscribe him within the limits of our fancy), but how much we admire him'.[1] Whether a word is 'significative of honour' is settled by convention. God should be worshipped in public as well as in private; but among a great diversity of public worshippers, each relying on his personal conventions, 'one would be apt to judge another's worship uncomely or impious'.[2] The sovereign must impose uniformity: those words 'which the sovereign ordaineth, in the worship of God, for signs of honour, ought to be taken and used for such, by private men in their public worship'.[3] Hobbes's nominalism also leads to religious authoritarianism, to a stark Erastianism.

§ 30 *How the sovereign is made*

A prerequisite for a public system of moral principles, then, is a supreme body, distinct from other bodies and easily identifiable; the allocation of moral names cannot be performed by anything vague and dispersed (such as popular sentiment or the general will); it must be done, not by a 'ghostly' body[4] which mutters indistinctly, but by a visible body which speaks decisively. Men must have 'the legislator known; and the laws . . . sufficiently published'.[5]

Not only the making of moral distinctions by the sovereign, but the making of the sovereign himself, is, for Hobbes, a curiously artificial and nominal process. Hobbes's nominalism grows—in conjunction with his psychology—into what may be called a nominalist theory of the state.

Consider, by way of contrast, Aristotle's realist theory of society, according to which families coalesce naturally into larger communities, because men have their essential properties

---

[1] *Lev* p. 191 & *EW* iii, p. 352.   [2] *De Cive* xv, 17 & *EW* ii, p. 221.
[3] *Lev* p. 192 & *EW* iii, p. 356.   [4] p. 171 & p. 316.
[5] p. 142 & p. 261.

in common and differ only in their accidental properties. A community is more than a 'mere alliance' of men;[1] it is a natural whole. Chronologically, there were men before there were political communities; ethically, a community 'is prior in the order of nature to the family and the individual':[2] the proper functions of its members are determined 'with reference to the goodness of the whole'.[3] The politicizing of men is an essentially natural process; political art should do no more than bring to a finish whatever nature has been unable to complete.

When Hobbes was writing in a political or religious context, his nominalism tended to be uncompromising. His nominalist ontology, uncompromised by 'accidents', precludes all talk of men having essential properties in common. If some people who, though unrelated, all happened to be called 'Smith', were in a room together, they would not coalesce into a *Smithian* whole; they would be just a collection of Smiths. If some creatures who are all called 'man' are on the same territory, they do not naturally coalesce into a human community. Without political organization they are just a multitude of men. Moreover, Hobbes's psychology positively implies that men 'are born unapt for society',[4] that nature dissociates men.[5] If men opt for organized society it is because

> they become at last weary of irregular jostling, and hewing one another, and desire with all their hearts, to conform themselves into one firm and lasting edifice.

And the contra-natural task of forming them into an organized political structure is a hard one:

> they cannot, without the help of a very able architect, be compiled into any other than a crazy building, such as hardly lasting out their own time, must assuredly fall upon the heads of the posterity.[6]

---

[1] *Politics*, 1280 b.   [2] 1253 a.   [3] 1260 b.
[4] *De Cive* i, 2 n. & *EW* ii, p. 2 n.   [5] *Lev* p. 62 & *EW* iii, p. 113.
[6] *Lev* p. 167 & *EW* iii, p. 308.

Hobbes insists that political unification is an artificial process,[1] imposed from above and brought about by terror.[2]

How does this process begin? How does a multitude of natural men set about turning itself into a single *people* or *body politic*? The short answer is: by instituting a sovereign to impose unity on them. But what does the creation of a sovereign involve? Does each man transfer something to him? If so, what is this magical gift, receipt of which can transform an ordinary human being into a mortal god?

Hobbes often appears to be saying that they transfer something occult and intangible to him—their powers, or their wills, or their persons, or their rights. But it becomes clear that what he writes in these veins, though suggestive of his underlying idea, is not to be taken quite literally. Thus he says:

> The only way to erect such a common power . . . is, to confer all their power and strength upon one man, or upon one assembly of men.[3]

But a man cannot literally confer his club-wielding strength or other powers upon another man.[4] Hobbes also says:

> When many wills are involved or included in the will of one or more . . . then is that involving of many wills in one or more, called *union*.[5]

But one man's will cannot literally be involved or included in

---

[1] *El of L* I, xix, 5 and II, ii, 4 & *EW* iv, pp. 121 and 140; *De Cive* v, 5 & *EW* ii, pp. 66–8; *Lev* pp. 1 and 87 & *EW* iii, pp. ix and 157.

[2] *De Cive* v, 8 & *EW* ii, p. 69; *Lev* pp. 87–8 & *EW* iii, p. 158. Hobbes had spoken of a body politic arising 'as it were naturally' (*El of L* I, xix, 11 & *EW* iv, p. 123); but by this he meant men submitting to a conqueror 'for fear of him', as opposed to their instituting a sovereign for fear of each other. Fear is still the motive.

[3] *Lev* p. 87 & *EW* iii, p. 157; and see *De Cive* v, 11 & *EW* ii, p. 70.

[4] 'It is impossible for any man really to transfer his own strength to another' (*El of L* I, xix, 10 & *EW* iv, p. 123).

[5] *El of L* I, xii, 8 & *EW* iv, p. 70.

another man's. Hobbes also says that men shall 'appoint one man, or assembly of men, to bear their person'.[1] How this should be understood we will consider shortly; here I will only remark that it, too, obviously cannot be taken literally. Hobbes sometimes speaks of each man giving up his right of governing himself to his sovereign.[2] This might be taken literally; but elsewhere Hobbes insists that there is no *transfer* of rights from men to the sovereign: men only renounce or lay down their rights; and

> he that renounceth, or passeth away his right, giveth not to any other man a right which he had not before. . . . The effect which redoundeth to one man, by another man's defect of right, is but so much diminution of impediments to the use of his own right original.[3]

Thus men do not literally transfer their powers, wills, persons or rights to their sovereign. But if the sovereign received nothing from them, he would possess no authority; for neither God, nature, nor the laws of nature single out any one man or body of men to be master over the others (see above, p. 46). He must have received *something* from them.

One of Hobbes's favourite ways of characterizing sovereignty is to say that the sovereign *bears the person* of his subjects. What, given his thorough-going nominalism, could Hobbes have meant by this? The answer which readily suggests itself is this: his subjects have given him, not their persons but tokens of their persons, *viz.* their *names*. And this is, in fact, what Hobbes meant. Each subject authorizes his sovereign to represent him '*or act in his name*'.[4] This is a familiar idea in English law: if John Doe gives Richard Roe unrestricted power of attorney, Richard Roe can sign legally binding documents 'p.p. John Doe'; John Doe agrees to regard acts done in his name by Richard Roe as if he had done them himself. For

---

[1] *Lev* p. 87 & *EW* iii, p. 157.
[2] See, for example, *Lev* p. 87 & *EW* iii, p. 158.
[3] *Lev* p. 65 & *EW* iii, p. 118; and see above, pp. 136-7.
[4] p. 80 & p. 148, my italics.

Hobbes, a sovereign is the representative of the men beneath him and they are the authors

> of every thing their representative saith, or doth *in their name*; every man giving their common representer, authority from himself in particular; and owning all the actions the representer doth.[1]

This nominalist theory of authority, according to which men authorize someone to act in their names and regard themselves as the authors of his acts, reconciles two of Hobbes's ideas which otherwise seem to conflict. On the one hand, the sovereign, once instituted, dictates the people's morality to them; on the other hand, he owes all his authority to the people, and the people continues, in some sense, to rule:

> The *people* rules in all governments. For even in *monarchies* the *people* commands.[2]

But it is only in a nominal sense that the people continues to rule. If John Doe, after giving Richard Roe power of attorney, goes on a long sea voyage, he continues in nominal charge of his affairs: transactions can still be done in his name. If his house is sold in his name by Richard Roe to Mrs. Roe for five pounds, John Doe will have to regard it as his own act. Hobbes would say that John Doe cannot, without absurdity, complain that he has been *injured* by what Richard Roe has done.

> Because every subject is . . . author of all the actions, and judgements of the sovereign instituted; it follows, that whatsoever he doth, it can be no injury to any of his subjects. . . . He that complaineth of injury from his sovereign, complaineth of that whereof he himself is author; and therefore ought not to accuse any man but himself; no nor himself of injury; because to do injury to one's self, is impossible.[3]

[1] *Lev* p. 82 & *EW* iii, p. 151, my italics.
[2] *De Cive* xii, 8 & *EW* ii, p. 158.
[3] *Lev* p. 90 & *EW* iii, p. 163. This idea that a subject is the author of all his sovereign's acts is hard to reconcile with Hobbes's attempt to justify a Christian subject's duty to obey a sovereign who commands him to deny that he believes in Christ. In *this* connection, Hobbes says 'that whatsoever a subject . . . is compelled to do in obedience to his sovereign . . . , that action is not his, but his sovereign's' (*Lev* p. 271 & *EW* iii, pp. 493–4).

Hobbes's nominalist theory of the state might be summarized thus: a multitude of men becomes a body politic when each of them gives to one (or a number) of them the free use of his name, so that the sovereign thereby created may, in the name of them all, allocate such names as *just* and *unjust*, *good* and *evil*, and cause men, by threat of punishment, to conduct themselves toward each other in accordance with the civil laws (and moral principles) thereby created. One can see why Cudworth (who lumped Epicurus with Hobbes) spoke of 'these artificial justice-makers, city-makers, and authority-makers'.[1]

[1] *TIS* iv, p. 201.

IX

Conclusion

Now we must collect the apples we have shaken from the tree. We have drawn various political implications from some of Hobbes's philosophical ideas, and we have found these political implications borne out in his civil philosophy. In § 31 most of these political implications will be assembled (references being given in parenthesis to the place where the implication was drawn) and presented as a summary of his civil philosophy. This summary will provide a sweeping solution for the political problems, indicated in § 1, posed for Hobbes by the Puritan Rebellion. We shall have come full circle. Our main task will be done. It will only remain to attempt an overall evaluation of this whole Hobbesian system of ideas. In § 32 I shall argue that just because Hobbes tried, unsuccessfully, to demonstrate his political conclusions, he succeeded in elaborating a richly criticizable political philosophy—which is what we should ask from a political philosopher. In § 33 I will indicate a few of the criticisms to which his political philosophy appears to be open.

§ 31 *Round-up of political implications*

His civil philosophy will set out from an account of men as they would be if civil society were entirely dissolved (p. 72). They are egocentric (pp. 110–11), restlessly ambitious (p. 115), and lonely: though their bodies collide, their minds never meet (p. 101). The scarcity of resources in a state of nature forces men to competitive strife; and competitive strife causes their

163

resources to be very scarce indeed (p. 103). They are imagined to be equipped with a moral vocabulary; but there are no objective moral properties to regulate its employment (pp. 150–1), no natural standards of good and bad (p. 45); their moralizing talk rather tends to intensify their conflicts (p. 151). No man is by nature intrinsically superior to any other man in any qualitative or ethical sense (p. 46); and although some men are physically stronger than others, it is an empirical fact that even the strongest may get killed by the weakest (p. 117). Every man faces the near-certainty of getting killed eventually, if he remains in a state of nature (p. 119); and while life lasts there is 'continual fear, and danger of violent death',[1] so that life in a state of nature is utterly miserable (p. 118).

Now a man's fear of violent death is stronger than any other fear, and it overrides any competing desire for pleasure (pp. 116–17). The laws of nature are assertoric hypothetical imperatives which prescribe conduct practically necessary for the avoidance of violent death (p. 83). They show men how to get out, and stay out, of a state of nature. By these laws each man is required to recognize other men as his equal (p. 117), and to agree with them to submit themselves to a single man (or body of men) who will speak with a single voice (p. 157). In so doing, they are both the maker and the matter of the body politic (p. 71). A body politic is a contra-natural artefact (p. 160) whose members authorize from below (pp. 73–5), their sovereign to act in the name of them all (p. 160) and to impose an artificial unity on them from above (p. 159). Unity requires, among other things, the imposition of an arbitrary but uniform style of religious worship (p. 157). Unity is effected by the enactment and enforcement of statute laws. There is no question of judge-made law being superior to the sovereign's statutes (pp. 38–40); for the latter create the distinction between just and unjust, right and wrong, good and evil (pp. 152–3); and it would be not merely seditious but preposterous for any subject (whether he be a private citizen or a judge) to impugn the justice or rightness of any of these laws (pp. 153–4). Provided they are not

[1] *Lev* p. 62 & *EW* iii, p. 113.

over-complex, so that subjects transgress them inadvertently, the sovereign's laws will not diminish the subject's liberty (p. 134). Transgressions of them will be punished—by death, if necessary—in a utilitarian and non-retributive spirit (p. 135).

The sovereign, however, is far from all-powerful. It is only men's outward behaviour which he should attempt to control (p. 97): inquisitions into their inner beliefs are futile (p. 102). And he may lose control of their outward behaviour: since men are bound to try to resist a threat to their lives (pp. 116–17), the sovereign will lose the allegiance of people whom he ceases (whether voluntarily or involuntarily) to protect (p. 137). He too is only mortal (p. 74).

It will be remembered that Hobbes attributed the Civil War to divided authority caused by ideological fever, the largest contribution to the latter being made by Puritan militants who claimed that their consciences obliged them to resist the civil authority, sometimes adding that they had experienced a personal revelation of God's instructions to them. We can see now that Hobbes could make a pretty brutal reply to such claims. Puritan ideologies, like other moralistic ideologies, are but inflated expressions of their spokesmen's personal ambitions (p. 151); in setting themselves up as judges of good and evil these men are vainly committing the original sin all over again (pp. 151–2); in calling existing laws unjust they are absurdly contradicting themselves (pp. 151–2); in claiming to know about God they claim to know about the unknowable (pp. 68–9); and in pretending to be divinely inspired they have put God for the cause of experiences which have local and undignified causes (pp. 109–10).[1]

As for Hobbes's own political prescriptions, his method ensures that they are not mere puffed-up expressions of his wants, but demonstrated theorems which can be denied by no one who is honest with himself, and who has worked out the logic

[1] 'Out of pride and ignorance, [they] take their own dreams and extravagant fancies, and madness, for testimonies of God's spirit' (*Lev* p. 205 & *EW* iii, p. 379).

of his situation (pp. 79 f.). And if a Christian reader should still demur, it may be added that these theorems, being deduced from the principles of our human nature, are also laws willed by God the author of nature (p. 95).

Hobbes's civil philosophy meets the first two of the desiderata stated on p. 16 above, for among its conclusions are: (1) men need an unlimited sovereign power over them; (2) in commanding subjects to do *x* the sovereign makes it their *duty* to do *x*. But did Hobbes meet the third desideratum? Did he *demonstrate* these conclusions? This we must now consider.

§ 32   *Demonstrability and criticizability*

Hobbes was gratified to be able to report that a French summary of his *De Cive* 'carrieth the title of *Ethics Demonstrated*'.[1] As we saw (p. 31 above), he regarded everything in *De Cive* except the arguments for monarchy as demonstrated. Towards the end of *Leviathan* he declared:

> And as to the whole doctrine, I see not yet, but the principles of it are true and proper; and the ratiocination solid.[2]

He hoped that a time would come when men ceased 'to prefer ancient errors, before [his] new and well-proved truth'.[3]

But for his political doctrines to be well-proved truths it was not enough that his principles should *be* true and his ratiocination solid. His principles would have needed to be *known* to be true. But how could they possibly be known to be true? *They* are not derived by ratiocination from superior principles. Hobbes hoped that they would be found intuitively obvious, rather as he had found Euclid's axioms intuitively obvious. But they go far beyond anything which might be known by intuition. Consider his key principle that men have an overriding fear of violent death. Now even if Hobbes could have known by introspection that he had such a fear, he could not be certain that men are uniform in this respect. Indeed, he

[1] *EW* vii, p. 333.   [2] *Lev* p. 394 & *EW* iii, p. 710.
[3] p. 394 & p. 711.

could not even know that *he* had such a fear; for the statement
that he did entails an infinite number of conditional statements
of the form: 'If Hobbes had had to choose between *x* and being
killed, he would have chosen *x*.' And in the course of his very
long and fairly eventful life Hobbes could have verified only a
finite number of these predictions.

Actually, it seems that this principle of Hobbes has been
falsified, and not just by stray counter-examples. In *The Golden
Bough* Sir James Frazer provided (though without explicit reference to Hobbes) what amounts to a *systematic* refutation of it.
The volume entitled *The Dying God* is concerned with kingships
among tribes which shared the magical belief that their martial
success and material prosperity depended on the virility of their
king: the belief that, if his powers declined at all significantly,
the rain would not come, or their cattle would sicken, or their
enemies would defeat them, etc. They held, consequently, that
a reigning king should be ceremonially killed, and his place
taken by a younger man, before an ominous decline set in.
Among some of the tribes, the ceremonial killing of the king
took place upon the appearance of the first tell-tale signs—a
tooth falling out, hair greying at the temples, sexual dissatis-
faction among the king's wives. Other tribes preferred to set a
fixed term—such as five years—at the end of which the king,
however fit, was killed or consented to kill himself. In some
cases the ceremonial killing was a gruesome business.

Among the evidence Frazer presents there is, as one would
expect, some confirmation for Hobbes's principle. Some kings
tried to break the custom. Sometimes a reluctant king had to be
compelled to take office; and in one territory (Ngoio, in West
Africa) where, to minimize the risk of a premature royal
decline, the rule was that the king should be killed on the night
of his coronation, the throne remained vacant.

Far more striking, though, are the many cases where a new
king came forward voluntarily, fully accepting that he would,
in due course, meet his predecessor's fate, and going quietly
when the time came. One of the witnesses quoted by Frazer
gave a vivid example of this. In Malabar there

was an office tenable for five years during which its bearer was invested with supreme despotic powers within his jurisdiction. On the expiry of the five years the man's head was cut off and thrown up in the air amongst a large concourse of villagers, each of whom vied with the others in trying to catch it in its course down. He who succeeded was nominated to the post for the next five years.[1]

This plainly conflicts with the assumption in which Hobbes's laws of nature were grounded, namely that power-hungry men will renounce their ambitions if they realize that they are almost sure to get killed in pursuing them. (It may be objected that the men Frazer was considering were sustained by a belief in the survival of their souls; but so were most of the men whom Hobbes was addressing.) In a chapter entitled 'The Supply of Kings' Frazer considered this strange-seeming willingness to be a doomed king. He claimed that it is not really so unusual, citing evidence from many parts of the world of mass indifference to, even eagerness for, death. His conclusion might be taken for a criticism of Hobbes:

> We shall never understand the long course of human history if we persist in measuring mankind . . . by the standard . . . of the modern English middle class with their love of material comfort and their passionate, absorbing, almost bloodthirsty clinging to life.[2]

Hobbes's system, if the reconstruction of it in this book has not gone badly wrong, ranks with those of Plato and Spinoza, at least for comprehensiveness and connectedness; but none of its political doctrines is proven, since none of its principles is certainly true, and at least one key principle seems to be false. Does this mean that Hobbes failed? Judged by the aim he set himself, the answer is, Yes. He failed to do what he set out to do, which was to found a demonstrable science of political duties. But then, anyone who sets out to do this is bound to fail.

Quoted in *The Dying God*, 3rd ed., 1930, p. 34.
[2] *Op. cit.*, p. 146.

How should we evaluate this interconnected system of ideas, all of them fallible, most of them controversial, and some of them outrageous? Among British empiricists, with the exception of Hobbes himself, there has been a strong tradition of hostility to *systems*. This tradition was started by Francis Bacon, who thought that philosophical systems blocked the *growth* of knowledge.[1] He regarded a philosophical system-builder as an intellectual authoritarian who tried to overawe his readers by making the parts of his system so reinforce each other that the whole seemed impregnable. He who wishes to advance knowledge does best, according to Bacon, to deliver his thoughts in the form of aphorisms; 'delivery by aphorisms' obliges a writer to stick to bare essentials, and allows each of his thoughts to be examined by itself, not supported by a fine-spun web of justifying reasons.

> Illustration and excursion are cut off; variety of examples is cut off; deduction and connexion are cut off.[2]

But is it really desirable that these things should be 'cut off'—in particular, that 'deduction and connexion' should be? The objective content of a theory or statement (as opposed to its psychological effect on people) is the totality of its logical consequences,[3] all that could be 'got out of' it.[4] The less one tries to get out of it, by logical derivation, the less one is likely to know of its content, and the less likely one is to uncover any questionable or objectionable content it may have.[5] Also, there may be strains, or plain inconsistencies, between it and other of one's theories or statements; and these are more likely to

---

[1] See, for example, *Novum Organum* I, aph. 67 & *Works* iv, p. 69, and *Filium Labyrinthi*, § 4 & *Works* iii, p. 498.

[2] *De Augmentis Scientiarum* VI, ii & *Works* iv, pp. 450–1.

[3] See A. Tarski, *Logic, Semantics, Metamathematics*, trans. Woodger, 1956, pp. 30 f., 40 and 62–3.

[4] See R. Carnap, *The Logical Syntax of Language*, 1937, § 14.4.

[5] So far as I know, it was K. R. Popper who first emphasized that logical derivation is important, outside mathematics, not for 'proving' or 'justifying' conclusions, but for criticizing premisses.

come to light if one systematically examines their inter-connections (negative as well as positive). Thus deduction and connection are important for internal criticism. They are also important for external criticism. If the contents of a string of aphorisms were organized into a deductive system, the critic would have one large target to shoot at instead of lots of little ones; and it would be easier for him to see where a hit would cause serious damage.

No doubt Hobbes was something of an intellectual authoritarian. But what matters is what a system-builder succeeds in doing, not what he set out to do. Provided he writes clearly and argues logically, as Hobbes did, his very attempts to justify or prove his conclusions will result in his presenting a more *criticizable* target; for a conclusion is 'justified' by being derived from a set of premises which has more content, and is therefore more criticizable, than it.[1] The more a system-builder succeeds in making parts of his system reinforce other parts, the greater the damage caused by the refutation of one part is likely to be. True, he may incorporate into his system a theory which condemns in advance all attempted refutations of it, or even, if it is sufficiently ingenious, enables defenders of the system to hail any attempted refutation as additional support for the system. But there is not, so far as I know, anything like this in Hobbes's system; and in any case, the exposure of such a defensive device would constitute a considerable criticism of the system which contained it.

What Hobbes provided, notwithstanding his tone of confident finality, was not a frozen block of political theory, but an immensely rich, criticizable system, open to revision and development at many points. Someone should do with Hobbes something like what Mach did with Newton. (It is sad that the one man who has tried to revise and develop Hobbes's ideas, R. G. Collingwood, was already a sick man when he began his

---

[1] A main theme of the striking series of articles, 'Proofs and Refutations', by Imre Lakatos (*Brit. Jour. Phil. Science*, May 1963–February 1964), is that a mathematical 'proof' usually opens up, contrary to its author's intention, ways of refuting the 'proved' theorem.

unsuccessful attempt.)[1] I will not attempt anything on this scale. I will merely indicate, in the next and last section, a few connected ideas in Hobbes's civil philosophy which seem most obviously to call for revision.

§ 33 *Taming Leviathan*

I shall select for criticism the following sequence of Hobbes's political ideas. (1) To avoid civil war, men must submit to a sovereign upon whom there can be no constitutional check whatever. (2) His subjects' liberty is not limited by laws which they feel constrained to obey. (3) The sovereign's laws are necessarily just. My criticisms will be quite pedestrian: in this area there is something to be said for keeping one's feet on the ground.

(1) We should applaud Hobbes's interpretation of the Civil War as the *un*intended outcome of the misconceived actions of ignorant men.[2] We may question, however, whether Hobbes attended sufficiently to the possible unintended consequences of *his remedy* for such unintended social disasters. An unlikely analogy may help to indicate the sort of thing I have in mind. Suppose that an economist, preoccupied with the problem of mass-unemployment in his country, successfully explains how it occurs although no one wants it, and how it could be eliminated, but ignores the possibility that his drastic remedy would cause international strains leading to retaliation and economic ruin for his country.

Hobbes did not altogether ignore the possible unintended

[1] In the Preface to *The New Leviathan*, 1942, Collingwood wrote: '. . . the almost incessant tempest through which we have precariously lived for close on thirty years has revealed Hobbes's *Leviathan* as a work of gigantic stature. . . . My own book is best to be understood as an attempt to bring the *Leviathan* up to date. . . .' (p. iv). Collingwood died in the following year.

[2] 'Not only from errors, but even from ignorance itself, there arise offences, contentions, nay, even slaughter itself' (*De Cive*, Pref. & *EW* ii, p. xi). See K. R. Popper, *The Open Society and its Enemies*, 4th ed., 1962, ii, pp. 94 f., for a rejection of the 'conspiracy theory of society' in favour of the view that the main subject of sociology should be the unintended consequences of human activities (including conspiracies).

consequences of his sovereign remedy; but he did not elaborate them. Instead, he gave the blanket assurance that, however bad they might turn out to be, they would be 'scarce sensible' compared with 'the miseries, and horrible calamities, that accompany a civil war'.[1]

Since we are now considering the validity rather than the reasonableness of Hobbes's ideas, we can invoke twentieth-century experiences of which he had little foretaste. He knew of only one political calamity (external wars excepted) besides which others pale into insignificance. We know of two: civil war *and totalitarianism*. And the question is whether his drastic remedy for civil war—an all-powerful sovereign upon whom there is no constitutional check—is not likely to lead to a situation as grim as the one it replaces.

Hobbes claimed that the interests of the sovereign and of his people broadly coincide: sovereigns can expect little delight or profit 'in the damage or weakening of their subjects, in whose vigour, consisteth their own strength and glory'.[2] Again:

> The good of the sovereign and people, cannot be separated. It is a weak sovereign, that has weak subjects; and a weak people, whose sovereign wanteth power to rule them at his will.[3]

In time of war this may be approximately true. But on Hobbes's own principles, one should rather expect a sovereign unconstrained by external exigencies to reduce the people to a paralysed state of fear and insecurity, at least if he enjoys the technological advantages of modern totalitarians. A sovereign is but a man; and 'men from their very birth . . . would have all the world, if they could, to fear and obey them'.[4] Like other men, he is supremely anxious to secure himself against threats to his person. If he is well versed in Hobbesian principles he will expect to be resisted by anyone against whom he proceeds. But if he is confident that his subjects are also well versed in Hobbesian principles, he can also expect to be resisted *only* by those he is actually attacking.

[1] *Lev* p. 94 & *EW* iii, p. 170.   [2] *loc. cit.*   [3] p. 182 & p. 336.
[4] *EW* vii, p. 73.

To resist the sword of the commonwealth, in defence of another man, guilty, or innocent, no man hath liberty; because such liberty, takes away from the sovereign, the means of protecting us.[1]

Thus, if his supreme ambition is to make himself as secure as possible and to have, if not all the world, at least all his subjects to fear and obey him, he may proceed to liquidate potential rivals and opposition leaders one by one, until he has effectively destroyed the possibility of organized opposition.[2] Then he can enlarge his operations, liquidating one by one those minorities which he regards as actual or potential obstacles to his ambitions. It may be objected that as his depredations increase so, on Hobbesian principles, will resistance to him. But he is operating against unorganized people; and each of his isolated victims can appreciate that, however bad his plight is now, non-compliance will make it worse. (If he refuses to dig his own grave he can be tortured to death. . . . The screw can always be tightened.) Eventually, such a totalitarian sovereign may reduce men to a condition of 'continual fear, and danger of violent death' not so different from that in a Hobbesian state of nature.

Hobbes might have replied that such a condition, though a risk under a sovereign, is a certainty in a state of nature; and that we must take the risk to avoid the certainty, *since there is no middle possibility*:

Sovereign power . . . is as great, as possibly men can be imagined to make it. And though of so unlimited a power, men may fancy many evil consequences, yet . . . whosoever thinking sovereign power too great, will seek to make it less, must subject himself, to the power, that can limit it; that is to say, to a greater.[3]

[1] *Lev* p. 112 & *EW* iii, p. 205.

[2] Hitler proceeded in this way, beginning with the Röhm purge. And something similar occurred under Stalin; about three-quarters of he members of central organs of the Russian Communist Party during 1917–22 came to a nasty end: see Leonard Schapiro, *The Origin of the Communil Autocracy*, 1955, p. 368.

[3] *Lev* pp. 106–7 & *EW* iii, pp. 194–5. Again: if the sovereign's 'power were limited, that limitation must necessarily proceed from some greater power' (*De Cive* vi, 18 & *EW* ii, p. 88).

Hobbes's argument is plausible: a political power can be limited only by a superior power; if there are two powers on the same level with no power above them—as were King and Parliament after the Non-Dissolution Act—a state of actual or incipient civil war exists. But we know now that a middle possibility does exist, that a sovereign body may be limited by something which is not a superior body: an elected body of men may enjoy unlimited legislative powers, yet face the possibility of dismissal at the next election. Hobbes emphasizes that Leviathan draws his original authority from below. We may add that his subsequent performance can be subject to periodic review from below.

A system of parliamentary sovereignty avoids the Hobbesian dilemma that a decision-taking authority can only be checked either by a rival body (= anarchy) or by a still more powerful body (= absolute sovereignty again). An 'electorate' is not a superior decision-taking body which gives orders to parliament from above. It cannot, ordinarily, initiate or veto parliamentary legislation. Nor is it a body which exists alongside parliament, sharing political power with it. It is not, ordinarily, an organized political body at all, only all the electors taken collectively. Yet its existence may effectively restrain the sovereign legislature.

A sovereign legislature is, of course, constitutionally free to prolong its own life, abolish elections, abdicate in favour of a dictator, etc. Several things may be said about this.

First, it is likewise conceivable that a Hobbesian sovereign may enact a constitutional law providing for an independent judiciary, representative assembly, periodic elections, etc. Within Hobbes's civil philosophy this would lead to a paradoxical situation. His theory of sovereignty involves the following two propositions: (i) whatever the sovereign enacts is just; (ii) the sovereign may not cede to another body any of the essential rights of sovereignty.[1] Since an unlimited sovereign power is free to enact that some of his rights shall be ceded to another body, (i) and (ii) may come into collision with each

[1] *Lev* p. 175 & *EW* iii, p. 323.

other;[1] for example, the Non-Dissolution Act was both *just* (a sovereign enactment) and *iniquitous* (destructive of sovereignty).

A supporter of parliamentary sovereignty would get into similar trouble if he were to maintain that a law is just if and only if it has been passed by parliament: he would not know what to think of a law, passed by parliament, transferring its law-making powers to a dictator. But there is no call for a supporter of parliamentary sovereignty to hold that any law is just if passed by parliament: he may hold merely that parliamentary sovereignty is, usually, the least bad kind of sovereignty despite the fact that parliaments sometimes pass bad laws. He may even hold without inconsistency that it is sometimes desirable for a sovereign parliament to exercise its sovereign right to prolong its own existence (as the British Parliament did in 1940).

(2) Hobbes's concept of liberty (see § 25 above) is often regarded as refreshingly commonsensical. That a man is free if he can do what he has a will to do is indeed more straightforward and less exploitable than the Rousseauist doctrine that he is free only when he obeys his 'real', as distinct from his actual, will. Yet certain implications of a rather sinister kind can be extracted from Hobbes's concept. It implies, it will be remembered, that there is no loss of freedom if external factors cause a man to change his endeavour and allow him to act out his new endeavour. Thus a law of the sovereign, as well as being automatically 'just', can cause no loss of freedom provided it is known and carries a penalty stiff enough to deter anyone from disobeying it. That much was already clear to Hobbes. Our modern knowledge of brain-washing techniques[2] enables us to discern further implications. Suppose that A and B are members of some underground organization in a totalitarian country, and that they have been caught. Each knows

[1] See K. R. Popper, *The Open Society and its Enemies* i, 7, §§ i–iii (and associated notes), for a proof that a theory of sovereignty such as Hobbes's —though Popper was not discussing Hobbes—is paradoxical.

[2] See, for example, William Sargant, *Battle for the Mind*, rev. ed., 1959.

that the secret police will try to extract from him the names of other members of the organization. Each is determined to withhold the names. The police decide to start with psychological methods; their aim is to get the prisoners to *want* to yield the names. Their methods work in one case, but not in the other: after a time, *A* gladly tells them all he knows, and is rewarded by a state job (perhaps in the counter-espionage section) which he afterwards performs diligently and contentedly (perhaps a chauffeur-driven car goes with the job). *B* defies both their psychological methods and their subsequent physical methods, and ends in a labour camp.

In one sense, *A* is indeed more free than *B*, as Hobbes's concept implies: *A* is doing what he wants to do, *B* is not. But there is an important sense in which it is *A* who has become a captive of the regime, and *B* whose soul has remained unenslaved, although he is now doing slave-labour. Hobbes's concept of liberty makes no provision for this sort of inner defiance.

(3) Hobbes's thesis that whatever the sovereign enacts is just (in conjunction with his thesis that there can be no constitutional check on what he enacts) leads, we saw, to paradoxes or inconsistencies, which is a sufficient objection to it. But it is worth considering how this thesis of Hobbes fares when subjected to a line of criticism which has often been deployed in this century against any such 'naturalistic' definition of ethical terms.[1] Applied to Hobbes, it would run as follows. A part of Hobbes's purpose was to *commend* the sovereign's enactments for their justice; but in attempting to guarantee that any sovereign enactment whatever is just he went too far and declared that 'just' *means* 'commanded by the sovereign'. For this verbal identification actually made him *unable* to commend sovereign enactments for being just; for when he *now* says that the sovereign's enactments are necessarily just, he says only that the sovereign's enactments are necessarily commanded by

[1] For this line of criticism see, for example, G. E. Moore, *Principia Ethica*, 1903, p. 14 and *passim*; and R. M. Hare, *The Language of Morals*, 1952, pp. 92–3.

the sovereign, a miserable truism: in trying to prove too much he defeated his own purpose.

But it is doubtful whether Hobbes would have been much shaken by this objection. It was on *prudential* grounds that he chiefly commended obedience to the sovereign. His opponents, on the other hand, tended to commend *dis*obedience on *moral* (or moral-cum-religious) grounds. Thus his reductionist definitions of 'just', 'good', 'right', etc., in terms of what is commanded by the sovereign, deprived him of a luxury he could afford to do without and his opponents of their main weapon— a worthwhile bargain.

No doubt Hobbes hoped, with his legal positivism ('no law can be unjust'), to endow the sovereign's acts with a moral aura; but this doctrine is really an extension of Hobbes's ethical scepticism. It is not because the sovereign possesses superior moral knowledge that his laws are automatically 'just' (any more than it is because he posseses superior theological knowledge that his interpretation of the Bible is automatically authoritative). Hobbes's sceptical conviction that there is no rational way of discriminating between competing moralities (or competing interpretations of the Bible) led him to conclude that an arbitrarily chosen system must be imposed and accepted *as if* it were the 'true' one. Hobbes's contention that the sovereign commands justly, whether he commands 'Thou shalt do x' or 'Thou shalt not do x', is feasible only on the sceptical supposition that we know nothing about the justice or injustice of x in itself. Behind Hobbes's legal positivism is the idea that private moral judgements are utterly subjective, that there are wild variations between the private moral judgements of different people, and that only harm results when the business of government is disturbed by moralistic clamour.

There are important elements of truth in all this. (I should warn the reader that from now on I shall do little more than aver personal opinions.) There surely is a subjective element in moral judgements; and political ideologies, inspired by high moral ideals, may create gratuitous political conflicts of a dangerous kind. Where a conflict can be resolved by appeal to enlightened self-interests, it is better so to resolve it, than to introduce provocative ideological considerations.

But there are political conflicts *no* resolution of which would be in the long-term self-interest of *all* the parties involved. Here, it seems to me, there is nothing for it but to attempt to find the solution which is least unjust or which has the least evil consequences. Moral considerations should enter where conflicts cannot be moderated by amoral considerations.

Saying this would be whistling in the dark if Hobbes's ethical scepticism were valid. Ethical scepticism is a large issue. I shall only offer a few unsupported comments on it here.[1]

There can be no proven or well-justified system of moral propositions. We cannot prove a moral proposition, or justify it in some weaker way, because the premisses of any 'proof' or 'justification' will be at least as unjustified as the original proposition. (The most one can do by way of justification is to show that a proposition follows from, or is supported by, propositions which one's audience accepts; but perhaps some of these have been *wrongly* accepted.) Recognition of this has led some justification-minded philosophers to conclude that there can be no rational discussion of moral principles: since they cannot be justified in any way, acceptance of them can only be the result of what are, logically speaking, sheer non-rational *decisions* (though, psychologically speaking, there need be no conscious decision-taking process: principles may be accepted unreflectively).

But it is a great mistake to infer that, since moral principles are unjustifiable, there can be no rational discussion of them. For the premisses of scientific theories likewise cannot be justified—cannot be verified or even be shown to be probable;[2] yet there can be rational discussion of them—because the intention is not to prove them but to *criticize* them, in the hope of uncovering inadequacies, and of replacing criticized premis-

[1] There is some support for them in a paper of mine in *Proc. Aristotelian Society*, suppl. vol. xxxvii, 1963.
[2] See K. R. Popper, *The Logic of Scientific Discovery*, 1959, especially appendix *ix.

ses by better ones. I believe that there can also be, and often is, critical discussion of moral principles. No doubt criticism in this sphere is less rigorous than it usually is in the scientific sphere; on the other hand, it may be less intricate and more down-to-earth: in a moral discussion, the number of independent propositions which are collectively under criticism is often relatively small, compared with the number under criticism in a scientific discussion; and the smaller the number of suspect propositions, the easier it is, other things being equal, to decide which are guilty.

If moral and political principles can be criticized, the moral and political principles of rulers and legislators can be criticized. My third criticism reinforces the first: rulers and legislators may be restrained by the existence of an electorate; and their policies and legislative proposals may be effectively criticized by electors and opposition groups.

I warned that my criticism of Hobbes's political ideas would be pedestrian. It could be summarized by saying that Leviathan may be more ferocious than Hobbes envisaged, and may be tamed in ways which Hobbes did not envisage. Hobbes is often regarded as having given a too pessimistic account of men, followed by a too draconian political remedy for their natural ills. *If* men were wolves, it is sometimes said, a Hobbesian sovereign would be the only remedy; fortunately, men are better than wolves. I think that this line of criticism concedes both too much and too little to Hobbes. If Hobbes's account of men is in some ways too pessimistic, it is also in some ways not pessimistic enough. Men can be much better than wolves; they can also be much worse.[1] I do not believe that men are essentially vicious. Nor do I share the view of the humanists of the Enlightenment that men are essentially good, the evil which

[1] I say this advisedly, in the light of Lorenz's account of the way in which the losing wolf in a wolf-fight asks for, and receives, mercy. He writes: 'I think it a truly magnificent thing that one wolf finds himself unable to bite the proffered neck of the other, but still more so that the other relies upon him for this amazing restraint. Mankind can learn a lesson from this. . . .' (Konrad Z. Lorenz, *King Solomon's Ring*, Intro. W. H. Thorpe, 1961, p. 197).

they do being the result of poverty, false teaching, and other external causes. I believe that our untutored human nature is, by itself, neither good nor bad but essentially *ambivalent*, that our deepest urges can spend themselves indifferently in good or bad, constructive or destructive, ways. If human co-operation goes far beyond anything analogous to be found in other species, so does our politically organized brutality.

If men are potentially much better and much worse than wolves, what they need is not some heavily repressive political apparatus which will clamp down indiscriminately on their ambivalent natures. For one thing, it is within authoritarian political regimes that some of men's worst tendencies come out.[1] They need civilizing traditions and institutions, a settled way of living and a social atmosphere which, while helping to train their ambivalent dispositions into decent habits of behaviour, will allow them to indulge their peculiarly human capacities for curiosity, invention and criticism, for conversation and laughter.

Recently, two propositions have been widely entertained among English-speaking philosophers. One is that philosophical ideas can have no implications for morals and politics. The other is there can be no rational discussion of top-level moral and political principles. I hope that this case-study shows that moral and political principles *can* be rationally discussed in the light of philosophical ideas.

[1] See the chapter, 'Why the Worst Get on Top', in F. A. Hayek's *The Road to Serfdom*, 1944.

Bibliography

The following works have been referred to in the main text:

Frithiof Brandt, *Thomas Hobbes' Mechanical Conception of Nature*, Copenhagen, 1928.

M. J. Oakeshott, Introduction to *Leviathan* (Blackwell), 1946; and *Rationalism in Politics*, 1962, pp. 248–300.

Richard Peters, *Hobbes*, 1956.

G. C. Robertson, *Hobbes*, 1886 (reprinted 1901). A pioneering study.

Leslie Stephen, *Hobbes*, 1904.

Leo Strauss, *The Political Philosophy of Hobbes*, 1936.

Howard Warrender, *The Political Philosophy of Hobbes*, 1957.

II Further works in English on Hobbes:

G. E. G. Catlin, *Thomas Hobbes, as Philosopher, Publicist and Man of Letters*, 1922.

G. P. Gooch, *Hobbes*, 1939 (reprinted in *Studies in Diplomacy and Statecraft*, 1942).

F. C. Hood, *The Divine Politics of Thomas Hobbes*, 1964. This appeared too late to be considered above. It goes further than Warrender's book in its emphasis on the Christian aspect of Hobbes's thought.

J. Laird, *Hobbes*, 1934. A work of considerable historical scholarship.

A. E. Taylor, *Hobbes*, 1908. An admirable little book, over-shadowed by the author's article in *Philosophy*, October 1938.

III There are substantial discussions of Hobbes in:

D. G. James, *The Life of Reason: Hobbes, Locke, Bolingbroke*, 1949.

C. B. Macpherson, *The Political Theory of Possessive Individualism: Hobbes to Locke*, 1962. A scholarly work written from a neo-Marxist standpoint.

IV There will be a useful collection of recent articles on Hobbes in:

K. C. Brown (ed.), *Hobbes Studies* (1965). This will contain Taylor's 1938 article.

V Contemporary reactions to Hobbes are discussed in:

John Bowle, *Hobbes and his Critics*, 1951. The author sides with the critics.

Samuel I. Mintz, *The Hunting of Leviathan*, 1962. An admirable book.

VI Bibliographies:

Douglas Bush, *English Literature in the Earlier Seventeenth Century, 1600–1660*, 1945. An invaluable work of reference, with a 170-page bibliography.

T. E. Jessop, *Thomas Hobbes*, 1960. Contains a bibliography especially useful for continental works on Hobbes.

Hugh Macdonald and Mary Hargreaves, *Thomas Hobbes, a Bibliography*, 1952.

VII   Out of the immense literature on the Puritan Rebellion I select, somewhat arbitrarily, the following:

> J. W. Allen, *English Political Thought 1603–1660*, vol. i *1603–1644* (all published), 1938. Does not mention Hobbes, but gives close analyses of political arguments going on in Hobbes's time.

> S. R. Gardiner (ed.), *The Constitutional Documents of the Puritan Revolution 1625–1660*, 3rd ed., 1906.

> Christopher Hill, *Puritanism and Revolution*, 1958.

> J. R. Tanner, *English Constitutional Conflicts of the Seventeenth Century, 1603–1698*, 1928.

> A. S. P. Woodhouse (ed.), *Puritanism and Liberty*, 1938.

Index